How To
More Cli

Val Falloon

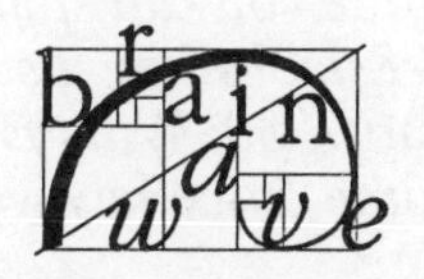

Cover design by Philip Buckley

Brainwave
BCM Raft
London WC1N 3XX

ISBN 0 9513347 5 1
Printed in Great Britain by BPCC Wheatons Ltd, Exeter.
Published September 1992

Contents

Personal Work 1

Marketing and Promotion 49

A Dedication

This book is dedicated to the 'Year of the Wood Monkey'. Monkeys are a lively and cheeky breed. They can be everywhere at once, do everything they set their minds to, and are skilful, inventive and adaptable. They have many faces, and enjoy being multi-talented, finding it hard to concentrate on one task only (however famous this might make them). Wood Monkeys, in particular, want life to be fun, and fun includes the wonder of self-discovery. They use their natural intelligence and their powers of observation (from being up above it all most of the time) to apply their discoveries to whatever happens to be going on, then they love telling everyone all about it. Some monkeys are even wise. Wood Monkey wisdom is based on the knowledge that unless we find the joy in life, we are done for. The universe can meet our needs, and half the fun is finding out where the particular bits we want are hidden. The other half is sharing all the goodies, and the remaining half is telling other people that they, too, can be Wood Monkeys: this year, everyone has been given permission to do this.

To discover ourselves, to revel in our multiple abilities, to explore how everything works, to develop new skills, to have fun, and most of to heal, is what being a whole person (and a Wood Monkey) is all about.

Wood Monkeys don't hang about on the nearest tree trying to get their message through to people who don't want to hear it. They pick up their boxes of tricks and set off through the jungle to find beings who are interested, and who want to know what they know.

Knowledge is power, and the greatest knowledge anyone can have is about themselves. Human beings (monkeys or not) are truly awesome, and this year I hope that everyone will allow themselves to believe that they can be everything that human beings are meant to be, and that they can find the route to everything they need within themselves.

Those who find this interpretation of Chinese philosophy somewhat liberal will perhaps have guessed that I am a Wood

Monkey (and a Gemini, which is like having a double dose of everything).

Having discovered (as I write) that we are destined for another half-decade, looking at it pessimistically, of a Government which continually penalises the self-employed, is dubious about natural therapies, and disapproves of anything that sniffs of individuality or human liberty, I have decided that the only way to deal with the last decade of the century is to have a good time and use whatever abilities I have to climb the tallest tree. The purpose of life is to live.

Who This Book is For

This book is for people who work with individuals or groups and who want clients, more clients, and a continuing flow of clients.

You may define yourself in one or more of the following categories: counsellor, holistic therapist, psychotherapist, complementary medicine practitioner, group facilitator or workshop leader. Or perhaps you are a healer, or a retreat leader, or the founder of a new religion. You may be considering opening your own natural health centre. You may be an experienced practitioner, or just setting up in practice. You may want to increase the number of clients you see, or explore new ways of working with a new client group or in a new settings. You may want to develop and sell products related to your therapy: books, tapes, oils, unique massage tables, overalls or diet books.

You are probably qualified in more than one discipline, or perhaps work in different ways with different clients, and could fit into two or three categories. The way you see yourself is more important to you than being described in someone else's terminology.

You treat your clients as whole people, and the only 'category' you find acceptable is holistic (or wholistic) therapist. You may, indeed, refuse any sort of categorisation or accreditation, because this would compromise your 'alternative' position.

This book is for you.

It is also for students and trainees. If you are about to start studying or have yet to choose a course, this book will help you clarify your training needs and to help plan your career. Your training may not teach you everything you need to know about the business end of setting up in practice, or about promoting yourself.

While this book is not specifically addressed to holistic businesses (such as retailers), the marketing concepts apply to any entrepreneur: the most successful of these have (even unwittingly) gone through all the processes detailed in this book.

Every one of us who chooses self-employment (for such is the lot of the 'alternative' therapist) has to tap into our inner entrepreneur. Fear not, you don't have to do it all alone. This book will give you all the information you need, and will help you to decide what you can do yourself, and where you need to ask for help from other people.

You will be pleasantly surprised to discover how much you can do yourself. The philosophy behind this book is that you can do everything you truly want to do with a little encouragement, advice or guidance from someone who has been through it before, together with the right sort of information. Most of the ideas in this book have developed as a result of personal experience.

I hope that once you try some of the things written about in this book that may be new to you, you will succeed. You will be hugging yourself with glee and saying 'I didn't know I could do that'.

What This Book Will Do For You

This book will:

- enable you to identify your motives for getting new clients
- show you how to identify your ideal clients
- help you to clarify why you are doing this work
- guide you through the mysteries of marketing and promotion
- ensure that your career plan harmonises with your life plan
- remind you of skills you had forgotten about, or now consider irrelevant
- prompt you to look at what you can do to help yourself
- encourage you to be clear about your own needs and to assert them
- dispel the fear that you are all alone, and that everyone knows much

more about all this that you do
- enable you to get more clients.

If the preceding prose reads like a rather elaborate workshop leaflet - well, it is supposed to. It is all part of the marketing 'process'. I am following one of the most important rules of marketing, which is to stress (subliminally, even) in your literature and other ways, the *benefits* of what you do, rather than the therapy itself. Potential clients want to hear what your therapy will do for them, not details of the theory of the therapy. For example; if you are a massage therapist, stress how massage will make them feel relaxed rather than how massage is done.

How This book is Structured

This book is in three parts.
Section I: Personal work- concentrates on you, your abilities, your needs and how your work fits into your lifestyle and personal growth process. It explains how working in a holistic way is an expression of you, and how using your personal process as a basis for your career development will enable you to find fulfillment in your chosen field. It will also help you to identify your ideal clients - the people who need what you uniquely offer.

Section II: Marketing and Promotion - is a complete guide to research, advertising, promotion, publicity and selling. It will help you to decide what you can do yourself, and what you may need help with. There are of different guide lines for different types of therapies and ways of working, and there are separate chapters on 'cross-over' subjects, such as workshops. This section will also reveal the mysteries of networking, the facts about the ubiquitous leaflet, and all those practical points you didn't want to tell anyone you didn't know about. It will show you exactly how to reach the people you want as your clients.

Section III: Resources is a resource directory of advertisers

It doesn't matter which section of the book you read first, though your choice will tell you a lot about yourself, or at least what your most pressing need is. That said, it it worth reading the book all the way through.

Marketing handbooks rarely cover the area covered in the section on personal work. For us, this is an important area because we are in a people business, one in which we create, hourly, new and necessarily close relationships with people. It is vital that the essence of you is expressed in your work. The term 'marketing', when applied to personal growth and therapeutic work, means getting yourself (as opposed to a product) across to the people who want what you have to offer. For this to succeed, you have to know who they are and, more importantly, you have to know who you are. Only then can you describe what you do.

It is sometimes impossible to separate your work from yourself, and for many people, their work constitutes much of their identity. This book puts the work in its place as one part of the pattern of your life.

Being aware of the connections between who you are and what you do, the reasons for the challenges life presents, and tapping into your limitless inner resources, will give you enormous faith in yourself, and the confidence to tackle whatever life has in store for you. Once you know how you function - how your particular process works - everything seems effortless and purposeful. You may enjoy clambering breathlessly over obstacles in order to experience the bliss of reaching the other side. Or you may find creative ways to get around them, or invent new methods which render the obstacles irrelevant. Or you may just do something for the fun of it.

Personal Work

Identity

Introduction

One of the most important factors in being successful is to be aware of what you uniquely offer. To some extent this is tied up with who you are as a person. So understanding more about who you are will help you define what you do that is unique.

Have you ever wondered why it is that some workshops, priced at £175, are fully booked months in advance, while others, at a bargain £45 (with concessions for the low-waged) attract a straggle of people at the last minute. Or why some natural health practitioners are doing typing or being bicycle messengers part of the time while others charge £55 an hour and work 40 sessions a week. Or why exceptional and inspired psychotherapists are debt-laden, while former community workers who have done a one year, part-time counselling skills course have six-month waiting lists. It is because they have discovered the secrets of promoting their unique skills.

What you offer is a unique service. You, and only you, have the set of skills you have as a therapist. You are unique, just like your clients are unique. Do not think of yourself as offering the same service as other therapists. No two homoeopaths offer the same service. Do not think of yourself as having gone through a production line training and have come out of it with the same skills as everyone else on the course. Who you are and what you offer is quite a different substance from a mass produced article on an assembly line.

This means that there is no real competition. I shall say that again. **There is no real competition.** You are unique. Your style of therapy is unique. Your clients are, each of them, unique. You do not have to compete with other therapists. Herein lies the simple answer to the question 'How do I get more clients?': *Realise what it is that you uniquely offer.* Then you can answer the other question: 'Do I actually *want* more clients?' (You see how simple it is?) Once you know what you *uniquely* offer, you only have one small challenge to face - marketing yourself. That is, *getting yourself across to the people who you want as clients.*

A Note For Students

If you are in training, or about to start your training, one of the questions you need to ask your (proposed) trainers is whether they will provide clients for you. Another question is whether they assess and select clients for you, so that you do not end up seeing people who you are not able to work with. Clients in search of therapists often contact training centres because they advertise frequently or have done considerable outreach work in the area. Clients are often provided by the training schools - the idea being that therapy is offered free or at very low cost. Training schools teaching complex therapies such as osteopathy, which are recognised by the NHS, follow allopathic medical school principles and have their own clinics where students can observe for some time before beginning to practice (literally) under the watchful eye of a teacher. Both the opportunity to practice as a student, and the possibility of clients being referred to you once you qualify, are important needs which should be met by the training school. If clients are provided to trainees and they also select clients for you then this is an enormous help in getting their trainees started. Some counselling courses, for example, find 'placements' for their students; others leave the students to find their own. Many newly-qualified practitioners form networks to share advertising costs and an answerphone.

If your training centre does not have this tradition, now is the time to start it.

Your first client

Facing your first client is a formidable business. Regardless of the amount of experience you gained during your training, going solo feels exactly like being on your own in the air without a co-pilot. Knowing the theory can give some succour when seeing your first client, but human interaction is so complex and varied leaving what may happen in the first session a large unknown. First-timers report a variety of problems, from small to enormous. Should I offer a client a cup of tea? Will the client actually turn up? What if I don't like, or feel afraid of, the client? How can I be sure the client will come back?

A recent survey in the USA found that 50% of psychotherapy clients did not come back after the first session. So don't be too upset if your client disappears. If you are finding that your first time clients regularly don't come back, it may be because they are picking up the fact that you need them more than they need you. Don't try too hard is the solution to this problem. Relax. Therapy (of any kind) is a two-way process, and the first session is, for both of you, a trial session. Go along with the view that you are finding out whether the two of you can work together.

Relax, breathe deeply, and concentrate on the work. Some people start in practice believing they must keep everything impersonal and clinical; others prefer to offer friendliness, good company and personal support. If you are concerned about personal safety (and many therapist are) either have an alarm button installed in your practice room, or only work within earshot of a colleague. If in doubt, never see a client if you are alone in the building.

Fear is what prevents you from getting and keeping clients, and fear is what prevents you from building your career. There are different sorts of fear of course. Personal safety is the most obvious one, fear of failure another, fear of not being loved and more often than not among holistic practitioners, fear of success.

Ways of dealing with these problems come with experience and trust in your own intuition. You may also need to build up a support network, which is dealt with later in the book.

Good luck!

Take Care of Your Needs

Before you start to build up your clientele be sure that you manage your own needs as you take on more clients. Many therapists rush headlong in the quest for more clients and successfully find them, only to end up a burn-out casualty. Many clients believe in the magic wand of the therapist and believe the therapist can heal him/her and do nothing wrong. It's fine if they believe this and it may become grist for the therapeutic mill. However, don't fall into this delusion yourself. It is safer to think of yourself as a frail person who needs care and nourishment. Those in the helping professions are notorious for not being able to look after themselves. For instance, psychiatrists have one of the highest suicide rates.

Look after yourself first and foremost, your clients come second. After all, if you can't look after yourself, how can you look after your clients? Recovering from burn-out is expensive, requiring time off work and extra holidays. A burnt-out therapist, on reflection, will see only a modest income over his or her last few years of practice and wonder whether it has all been worth it. Pacing is important. As you take on more clients consider a support network, supervision, effective scheduling, advance planning and time off. Remember that practitioners usually have no training in running a business and time is required to aquire business acumen. If you intend to be successful, much of your time will need to go into marketing and promotion. Make sure that the costs involved in this is reflected in the fees you charge your clients.

The first step in getting more clients is to identify what you want for yourself. Becoming a natural health practitioner or even a great guru does not guarantee immunity from life's little tests of your sense of humour, though it may help you be more philosophical about wars, deaths, disasters, the vanishing ozone layer, elections, recessions, etc etc. (one can always ponder the beauty of the omelette or become the world's first Professor of Entropy). Most people find, to their dismay, that being on a long training course results in a complete life change - a true Dark Night of the Soul, and many therapists start their careers with a great deal of unfinished business clogging their psyches. (Nobody tells you this when you part with a large cheque at the beginning of the course).

Considering that most of us are wonderful at guiding people along their chosen path in life or fixing their ills, it is ironic that we sometimes cannot do this for ourselves. We put our energies into our work and our training, and often forget about our own needs, perhaps gritting our teeth and saying: 'This person a lot worse off than I am, therefore I must be OK'. This is, of course, nonsense. You cannot meet anyone else's needs for very long unless you know how to meet your own.

One advantage that psychotherapists have over other practitioners is that our training requires us to experience the same therapeutic process ourselves, and professional recognition requires us to have lifelong personal support, called 'supervision' (though this is not, in any sense, 'managerial'). No counsellor or psychotherapist would want to be without it. We do, therefore, have a regular reminder that we too have needs. Practitioners without some kind of professional support, or membership of a peer group or network, usually rely on their own inner burn-out detector (which fails well before they do). Many body therapists now study counselling skills and form themselves into supervision and/or support groups, often with a professional facilitator. Much of what I will be exploring in this guide is about setting your own limits, and knowing when you need help or support is one of these.

If your primary need at present is money, then your motives for taking on new clients are going to be very different from someone whose belief is that when you are doing what you want, the money will flow in. Therapists who work with a whole-person approach know that they are whole people too. However, financial pressures often mean putting your needs on hold for a while and taking on work that isn't exactly right for you. If you are doing this, now is the time to re-draw your life plan, looking again at your ambitions, re-assessing your personal targets, and seeing how the taking on of new clients will fit into your scheme of things. You may indeed be enjoying the hurly-burly of mass-production. On the other hand, this may be the time to start phasing out. Nothing is more frustrating than committing yourself to renting a room for a year, or to ten new clients for two years, and then finding you are unable to accept offers to teach (for example) and have no time to attend courses or hold workshops.Talking of workshops - and there will be much more about these in Section II - the fact that they have to be planned at least nine months in advance means that you have to be very sure that doing a workshop nine months hence is just what you will feel like.

Look first at your *personal* needs - home, relationships, leisure, health, self-nourishment, travel, study, working abroad, as well as your *professional* needs (the more ambitious you are, the greater your support structure will have to be). Is getting more clients an end in itself, or a means to an end? Have you got (or can you get) enough love and healing coming in to you in order to give out more to your new and present clients? Are you living, or are your clients living your life for you? Do you have enough personal assets to cope with considerable change and greater demands on your psychic energy? Do you feel sure enough of your boundaries to be able to switch back into being you, the person, at the end of your working day? What effect will increased work time have on your relationships and your other interests? Will you need to take longer holidays? All these points, and many more, need to be given careful thought.

Whilst you can do some assessment of where your business is now and where you want it to head, it can be useful to enlist others in your planning. If, for example, you have been working for a long time and seem unable to increase your client list however hard you try, this may mean that you have 'grown out of' this particular way of working. You could have a brain-storming session with colleagues as well as a thorough self-assessment. You may, for instance, have decided that the way to get more clients is to hold more workshops. If so, here are some questions to ask yourself: as a workshop leader are you able to work alone, or would you prefer a co-leader? Could you cope with 30 needy people by yourself? Or would you prefer a group of 12, all at similar stages of self-awareness? What sort of room do you feel most comfortable in - a quiet attic or a community hall? A centre which you know, and which the public know hosts good workshops, and which mails out regular brochures? Your own home? a residential? abroad?

And who are you? Do you perceive yourself as an authoritative and charismatic leader, or a low-key guide offering a more supportive role? How do you deal with challenge, with hecklers? Do you want a 'talky' workshop, or is it better for you if people are quietly drawing, or meditating? Will you set them all beating cushions with baseball bats and hope for the best? Can you switch your attention easily to deal with individuals? Do you want people to split into small, self-managing groups? Would you know what to do if someone has a panic attack? Or, indeed, a rebirth? Can you think on your feet, or do you feel safer with a tight structure? Do you want to do lots of different workshops, learning as you go, or stay with the same basic workshop for several years?

Natural health practitioners have very different needs from, say, psychotherapists. A masseuse working in a City gym may never see the same client twice. Homeopaths, acupuncturists, or osteopaths may need to see clients regularly and sometimes over long periods, and long-term clients will come to view you as a counsellor as well. If you don't want this to happen, do you want to restrict treatment to, say, six sessions and refer on? If you practice shiatsu, aromatherapy or kinesiology can you cope with the memories and feelings that will result from the freeing of long-held blocks and the erosion of armouring? All treatments have different effects on different levels. The gentlest of touch therapies can create sudden stress, memories returning can create tight throats or headaches and spiritual practices produce considerable emotional discharge. Meditation gives some people headaches at first, and extended chanting can cause panic attacks.

These effects cannot always be anticipated by client or therapist. If you know you won't cope, will you warn clients what they might expect? If you give them a phone number for checking back with you if there are any problems, could you cope with late-night distressed phone calls? Do you have a network of colleagues you can refer clients to?

If you set your personal boundaries clearly (if only to yourself) you will be able to deal with these problems (and it is quite worrying how few training schools prepare their students for these possibilities, especially short courses).

Group facilitators are different again. An ongoing group can be 50 people for three years, or six people for 12 weeks who then go on to form a self-help group. Which would you prefer?

Discovering Your Vision

If you are doing what you want, life becomes easy, even efforless. If you are working in a job that you dislike then it's tough, life becomes dull and boring. Boredom kills, enthusiasm inspires. When you are truly doing what you want, then you will have energy and enthusiasm and work will become effortless. If your work is in accord with the inner you, then this is the successful ingredient to becoming a successful practitioner. You are not doing your job just for the money, otherwise you would be an accountant or plumber. You were attracted to the kind of work you are in for your own reasons. So it is important to know how you came to be doing it, and to understand your motives. You will then be in a position to know what it is you want and you will be more able to communicate this to others, especially your potential clients.

Individual motives for becoming a holistic practitioner of course vary hugely. There are no doubt as many motives as there are practitioners. Some are 'in it for love'. Some are in it because they meet such interesting people, or because they learn so much about themselves from their clients and colleagues, or because relationships with colleagues are so much easier than in the nuts and bolts business. Others are in it because the therapy worked for them. Others again because of the status it brings and the high of a hundred people humming when you say hum. Others because they like doing what they do and there was no real decision to be made. Some want to teach others their unique philosophy of life. Others, usually those who are extraordinarily gifted, have no choice but to share their gifts (usually these people are hopeless about asking to be paid). Some, let it be said, are in it because they are rescuers and need to work with with the needy. Yet others - the evangelist type - are in it for power and are most certainly not reading this, being the sons and daughters of gods and goddesses and therefore needing no guidance from a humble earthling such as me.

Let us assume that most practitioners do the job they do because they feel is is a good job, and that it enables them to express themselves creatively, that they enjoy the equality, the giving/receiving aspects of all healing work, that they enjoy contributing to the progress of the human race and accept their part in the universal scheme of things.

Once you have clarified why you are a therapist, you will have a better picture of where you are going from now. Look at the indicators of what you gain from your work. Is how you feel about yourself dependant on what your clients are doing, how your workshops went, whether your book is selling, or how many hugs you got today? Also look at what you *don't* get out of your work. It is important to be brutally honest with yourself: authenticity sells - people wanting to buy something (even in a sale) check for holes and hold it up to the light. Your clients will do the same with you - you won't be able to fool them. So, if you are in this business for power, status, money and fame - fine, as long as you are not pretending to others that you are in it for love, or because your guides told you to do it, or as some form of martyrdom.

This kind of self-assessment, which needs to be continual (a requirement incidentally, for counsellors and psychotherapists) is most important and most helpful in your moving-forward process. You may be wonderful at teaching others to live and incapable of getting your own life together. Perhaps you sit in envy as clients heal themselves and discover their life purpose, or stride out of your workshops with fire in their eyes, while you stagger home exhausted to a lonely microwave dinner and a Radox bath. There is also something to be said in the definition of work as 'other people's time'.

To market yourself effectively you need to be clear about what it is you do, which should stem from what you want. If you are not clear about what you want, you are going to be incapable of getting yourself across to the clients you want. Nobody out there will know who you are. Listen to what your inner voice tells you - you are the only one who knows the answer.

I have not defined 'work'. I am writing this in the Year of the Wood Monkey, in which, as I have proclaimed in the introduction, multi-skilled people will emerge and be applauded. So although 'work' is usually what you do in order to earn money, it is not actually important *what* work you do as long as the essence of you is being expressed in it. If you can whittle down all the preceding questions and concepts into one single quality, you will not feel despairing if you are unable to achieve your defined target or the purpose of your training. Some key 'life concepts' to look for are: communication, teaching, guidance, healing, promoting client empowerment, humanism, witnessing growth, being loved and appreciated, being admired, creativity, influencing people, leadership, contributing to human evolution...no doubt you can identify a core concept and relate it to your work.

The function of your personality is to express your inner self, not to hide it.

If you find that the reasons for being in this work have very little to do with you, then what is driving you? Your family? Your community? Escape? Who are you hoping to please, if not yourself? Who do your clients represent to you? If you are reading all this in order to find out why you are not getting enough clients, nor earning enough money, then it is even more important that you carry out a step-by-step self-assessment. If being a practitioner is not at all what you expected, you don't have to stay a practitioner. You can use what you have learned in a hundred other ways.

Clarifying What You Do

When potential clients ask you what sort of therapy you do, they are also asking: 'What will it do for me?'. It is important to sell the *benefits* of what you do rather than a description of what you do. Salespeople are constantly told to sell what the product will do for the customer, not a description of the product: 'these boots will enable you to climb the toughest of hills, will keep out the rainwater and impress your friends' is better than 'these boots have one inch thick soles, are waterproofed and have a nice shine to them'. The same applies to what you offer: 'Gestalt therapy will help you become aware of how different parts of yourself are in conflict and bring harmony into your life' is better than 'Gestalt therapy relies on the belief that the whole is more than the sum of the parts'.

You need to be clear about what you offer and to communicate this effectively to potential clients. Otherwise you will end up with dissatisfied clients and you will be dissatisfied yourself. Communicating what you offer, however, can be people are confused about the different therapies on offer; also, potential clients carry their own preconceptions. The key is to be clear that what you offer is unique. How is what you offer different from another therapy? How is what you offer different from another practitioner who practises the same therapy? Answering these questions helps you to define what you do. You are then better able to communicate this effectively to potential clients.

There are some assumptions you can make about clients' expectations. The cognoscenti will know the difference between physiotherapy, chiropractic, cranial osteopathy and postural integration. New Age seekers are usually willing to try anything new. Many people will try what their friends (or a columnist) have said worked for them. People who understand what 'complementary' medicine means will expect to hop from homoeopathy to aromatherapy to psychotherapy and perhaps to a healer and an astrologer. Many have specific 'groups' of therapies that they use, which depend upon their own belief systems and their lifestyles. (Other therapists are usually the most willing to experience different therapies).

Only you can decide which therapy or therapies you offer. If you are only qualified in one therapy and have developed this in a very personal way, you can preface the therapy with an adjective, such as 'remedial' massage or 'intuitive' massage. The best understood therapies are those which describe exactly what goes on, such as rebirthing and aromatherapy. So if you want to invent a new word for what you do, try and make it self-explanatory.

People new to natural therapies will not always know the differences (and some of them are extremely shall we say subtle) between the hundreds on offer. Some centres have addressed this by having consultants to explain to callers what is what. Sometimes they advise on specific therapies for certain conditions which directly addresses the clients' question. It is no good answering it by saying 'it works for everything.' No one can say that one therapy is better for rheumatism than another or that herbal medicine is better for panic attacks than behavioural therapy. What works for whom is dependent upon the individual; their personality, the way they deal with stress, how they perceive and exhibit symptoms and their willingness to view themselves as self-healing beings. If a potential client phones you, and after discussion you both decide that what you offer is not right for him/her, then refer him/her on. You may have reciprocal arrangements with other practitioners for this eventuality, or if not, then a handy copy of *The Whole Person Catalogue* will answer callers' questions.

Bearing in mind that the real question is 'What does it do for me?' it may be best to describe your therapy in these terms, stating how it works, what it can do, what it works well for, and its immediate effects - such as 'relaxing', 'energising', 'stimulates the body's immune system' or 'releases emotional blocks which cause illness', or simply that 'it makes you feel good'. Some treatments are not treatments at all, but techniques aimed at the prevention of various disorders. And, returning to the main point of this book - how you describe your therapy again depends on what you want to offer and the clients you want to attract.

There are people who want to be 'treated' or 'cured' and there are people who want to be tended and heard, so it is a good idea to make clear which group your therapy falls into. For example, osteopathy is more of a treatment than Shiatsu; the latter requires a willingness on the part of the recipient to experience surges of feelings; nutritional therapies need the active participation of the clients in changing their dietary habits; psychotherapy requires that clients 'work' on themselves between sessions. Reflexology is a treatment, while massage is seen as relaxing or indulgent. People coming straight from years of allopathic medicine are unclear about these differences and usually unsure about therapies which require a considerable change in their lifestyle - they are more likely to start with a therapy they perceive as a 'treatment'. Even then, with homoeopathy for example, they make not like the idea of giving up coffee or other strong-flavoured foods for two weeks while taking the remedy.

Probably the most difficult therapies to explain to clients are counselling and psychotherapy. There are endless categories, from astrological or psychic counselling to addiction recovery or relationship counselling, and by no means all of them use a holistic approach. Counselling is not a 'treatment', despite curious stories in the popular press about people being 'so traumatised that they had to have counselling'. Sometimes counsellors tend to work with the specific problem they were trained to work with: bereavement, substance dependency, psychosexual problems. To add to the confusion, many psychotherapists call themselves 'counsellors' because the word is less threatening to people who have had bad experiences of the NHS mental health system. Then there are different types of counselling, such as person-centred, pastoral, career guidance, psychosexual or psychodynamic. Then there are the named schools - Gestalt, T.A., Psychosynthesis, Feminist and hundreds more (around 300 at the last count).

In the end, the approach matters less than the personality of the counsellor, as long as he or she is clear about what they are qualified to offer - a counselling skills course provides little theoretical training, or any training on the application of the skills to specific problems. There are indeed people describing themselves as 'counsellors' who have done no counselling training at all, and little or no work on themselves. That said, it is frequently argued that you cannot go on a course to learn intuition. In psychotherapy, the position becomes even more complex, as there is intense competition and often rivalry and distrust between the major schools of practice - analytical, humanistic, existential or the spiritual approaches, though I must add that those in the latter categories are a great deal more accepting and broad-minded than those in the first.

If you are not clear about what you do, you will be working with clients that you do not want. And as well as being able to describe what you do, it is important to describe the way that you work. A hundred people with identical qualifications will work in 100 different ways. Will you require a full medical history? If so, will you ask clients to bring this with them? If you are a body therapist, do you work silently or with music? Do you tune in to your clients first? Do you do all the work, or do you expect your clients to participate or at least feed back to you what is happening? As a counsellor or psychotherapist, do you listen, feed back and summarise? Or do you use several techniques which encourage the physical expression of feelings? Do you prefer working with the unconscious or the imagination, with dreams and/ or visualisation? Do you include body work? Do you interpret or confront frequently? Are you talkative or quiet? Do you prompt or ask direct questions? Do you wait for your intuition to give you a clue and share that with your client?

The way in which you work will tell you what sort of clients you want. If your intuition requires silence and the client is chatty and wants music, little will happen. If your therapy requires a certain level of self-awareness and the client has none, it is going to require hard work and patience on your part.

If you need more clients in order to earn more money, or perhaps to have enough case histories to qualify, you will be tempted to say 'yes' to everyone. (Some would say this is a good learning experience). However once you are in a position to choose remember it is your choice.

This chapter has been specifically addressed to one-to-one therapists, though it also applies to people who teach, take groups, run workshops or, indeed, run centres. The idea of working in a holistic way is to be happy, or at least reasonably content, particularly if your purpose for being in this work is job satisfaction.

The happier you feel, the better you will do your work, and the more clients you will have.

Identifying Your Type of Client

When you have a clear idea of what you want and what you offer the next stage is to profile the clients who need those skills you have. Here it pays to be specific. Hone down the type of client who needs your skills. You may end up with something like this: 'I want to work with women who have difficulty expressing their anger and I want to help them overcome this block and to discover a new side to themselves. I want them to be committed to working on themselves and I want them to come regularly to sessions'. The following stage is to find these clients. Finding these clients is not as hard as it might appear. What's important is to know what you are looking for. Both profiling clients and finding them are handled later in this book under 'Marketing'. In this 'Personal' section the focus is on who you like to work with.

You may already know who your potential clients are. Perhaps, for example, the type of training you have had may already identify your particular sector of the community. For instance, tube commuters with dislocated shoulders from strap-hanging. It may also be that your training and professional association Code of Ethics and Practice limits the nature of the conditions you are qualified to work with. For instance, the International Society of Professional Aromatherapists recommends that practitioners limit themselves to treating chronic, rather than acute, conditions. You may also know from your existing clients, the type of people (as opposed to problems) you prefer to work with. For instance, those who seem to reflect different aspects of you, or who stretch you, or through whom you discover a great deal about yourself (including your formidable knowledge and abilities).

If as the weeks wear on you feel you are not using your talents much, or even your training, then you are working with the wrong clients. None of us are static, nor are our clients. They grow and change and so do we, so our needs change as well. Perhaps you have already determined your optimum working level and identified your ideal client: your next step, marketing yourself, will be considerably easier. If things are going swimmingly, you may only need let people know you are looking for more clients.

If you are not quite sure who your potential clients are, or have not been working for long enough to know, there are several ways of finding this out. As this is the Personal Work section, the following is about how you relate to your clients. In Section II, you will find detailed descriptions of how to make your selections in marketing terms. Meanwhile, here are some starting points.

Be aware of a time when you were completely in tune with a client, breathing with the same rhythm, a sense of giving and receiving, doing powerful work, and feeling energised rather than exhausted at the end of the session. Can you identify what it was about this client that resulted in this connection? What was their personality type - airy, fiery, watery or earthy, or a combination? What other ways could you describe this client? Young and courageous? Needy and insecure? A stoic? Creative? A vegan? Chatty and curious? Intuitive? Good boundaries and a high level of self-awareness? Trusting? Heavily armoured? Intellectual and challenging of you? Full of love or full of pain? What is it about them that struck a chord in you? Probably they were very like you, regardless of age, gender, lifestyle, class or ethnic origin - we are all much more like each other than we realise.

Perhaps you simply loved them. However hard one tries, one cannot love everybody. As love is rather an important factor in healing work (at the very minimum you need to care for and be interested in your clients) it is also important to know who you don't want to work with. In addition, if you have prejudices against certain groups of people then it is unwise to work with them. Prejudice is about fear and as fear makes you vulnerable and unreceptive, it blocks your ability to assert yourself and to remain in touch with your intuition. It is important to work on these prejudices of course, since they limit your choice of clients, and finding out why certain types of people repel you is in itself valuable.

Allow for the fact that clients may be considerably more damaged and needy than your friends, though for some people this is not always the case. That said, remember that even very damaged and needy people will have developed phenomenal skills, and they may be using these in negative or self-destructive ways because they don't recognise them as 'coping skills'. (Your favourite job may in fact be turning around their belief system so that they use these abilities for themselves rather than against themselves.)

So who are your potential clients, or should I say 'working partners'? Having worked out the type of people that they are, what do you want from them in order to help make your sessions go well? Do you want them to have a good knowledge of your type of therapy, or little knowledge about any type of therapy? What amount of work will you require them to do? Are you better at working with people who identify themselves by their problems, or those who see life as a series of challenges and are committed to a path of personal growth?

The more you know about your potential clients the easier it will be to find them: you will know where they are and you will be able to speak to them in their personal language. Be discriminating - in the original and positive sense of the word.

Work Place Options

Working in a Natural Health Centre

There are obvious places where clients will go to find you, and if you are at the beginning of your career, it makes sense to work in one of these places.

If the centre supplies the clients, then fine, you will have a steady supply of clients, the advertising is done for you, there are usually reception (if not bookings) services, and somebody else orders the supplies. If you do not yet have enough clients to rent a room every day, it is worth working in a centre, even at a loss, for one day a week, and moving clients you know well to your home as your list builds up. Though some centres may not like you doing this.

If the centre rents out rooms only, but will not help you find clients, you will need to find the rent of the room while you build up a clientele. This can be expensive and there is no guarantee that you will find sufficient clients there. Try to get your name in the promotional literature of the centre and to put your own brochure in their mailouts. You will need to promote yourself quickly in the locality. Indeed it is best to do advance promotion *before* you rent the room if possible. Make sure you meet the other practitioners at the centre and tell them what you do. They may well refer clients to you, just as you may do for them.

There is also a matter of your credibility when you start in practice. Clients coming to a reputable centre know that the practitioners will be of a certain standard (and if the centre does not ask you for copies of your certificates and your insurance policy, don't work there). Also check that the equipment meets the required safety and hygiene standards, and that all necessary pharmaceutical and cosmetic storage bye-laws are adhered to. Being in a centre which feels healing and professional has a positive effect on you and the way you work with your clients, as well as giving them confidence in you. You will also have referrals from the other practitioners, and indeed, some of them may become your clients (another plus to working in a centre - you can book a session with the on-the-spot aromatherapist if you or she get a cancellation. Or even if you don't.)

Sharing rooms or offices

If the busy-ness of a centre does not appeal, you may prefer to rent a couple of rooms with a colleague. Try your local natural health food store, bookshop or similar. They may have spare rooms above the store, and would not be as expensive as a centre because would not provide any of the services. A supportive or, at the very least, an understanding environment is essential. There is also something to be said for four or five practitioners renting a house together, in which case you need to have worked out a foolproof co-operative business plan. Bear in mind another aspect of working from a house: you will probably need to apply for 'change of use' planning permission.

If you are renting office space, you may find that you cannot have access at weekends (nor, in some cases, in the evenings).There is also something spooky about being the only person working in an office building in the evenings.

Clinic or health centre?

Where you work also depends on the type of therapy that you do. For example, if your therapy is a treatment, you may prefer to work in a centre which is known as a 'clinic' rather than a 'holistic health' centre. If you work one-to-one and with groups, it is helpful if your chosen centre also has a larger room for occasional hire to save you travelling time. Some centres have a 'New Age' clientele, and so advertise services in quarterly personal growth magazines or network bulletins read by known users of such a services. If you want to bring your therapy to a new or wider public, you may prefer a centre which regularly advertises in widely accessible publications, such as listings magazines or the local newspaper, and has occasional 'open days'.

An important factor to consider is opening hours. Clients will want evening and weekend appointments; you may want to hold evening classes or weekend workshops. Most commercially minded centres stay open until 9 pm during the week, and are open all day Saturday. In some there is the possibility of Sunday appointments though you may be responsible for opening up and locking up, and be alone in the building with your client. However, there are some 'clinic' type centres which are only open until 5.30, and not at weekends. If you are thinking of starting your own centre in a mixed office building (for instance) or local council 'seed bed' premises, there may be restrictions on the hours that the public are permitted in the building. The lease and buildings insurance policies will give you this information. Remember that there are different requirements in terms of licensing for 'clinics' and 'health centres'.

Working with doctors

GP's are more open to natural therapies than they were in the eighties, and several hundred GPs themselves now study acupuncture, homoeopathy or hypnotherapy. Many group practices have an in-house counsellor and some of these are paid by the practice, though you may have a limited choice over the clients you see or they have no choice at all. There is a scheme for GPs to be able to pay natural health practitioners for what they call 'clinics'. In other words, sessions for patients on preventive techniques or diet. It is best to approach GPs from a medical perspective, stressing symptom treatment such as stress management, breathing techniques for asthmatics, low-cholesterol diet counselling, exercises to ease chronic back pain, nutrition advice, pre-natal yoga and similar 'clinical' subjects. If the practice hasn't budgeted for an in-house 'clinic', you have at least made contact and the GP may refer clients to you.

Working in a mixed practice or community centre

Each centre has its own character, and it is important that you feel comfortable where you work. However, your first consideration has to be any restrictions your professional association places on working environments. Some codes of ethics make it clear that working with people who are not recognised as 'professional' brings disrepute to your own practice, and being in the wrong type of centre, with the wrong type of entrance can also mean a breach of the code. Some practitioners are more mutually compatible than others.

Natural health practitioners and body psychotherapists seem to work well together in a centre. Other practitioners who see clients on a long-term basis, especially counsellors, psychotherapists, rebirthers or homeopaths find that their needs are very different from those of, say, a colour healer.

This particularly applies in a community centre, where many of the workers will be part-time volunteers, who may not be trained counsellors and so cannot be expected to understand the nature of boundaries and the requirement for confidentiality. Your home telephone number will be filed by the centre staff who may need to be given instructions about who you want this to be given to.

Although rooms in community centres are often free, you will probably find you are only permitted to charge very low rates and may even have to see a certain number of clients for free. Or you may be limited to seeing clients in the neighbourhood which the centre serves. However, since most of these centres are constantly under-funded, they might welcome creative suggestions from you about boosting their revenue. Perhaps you could arrange to take the room for an extra number of hours as a private hire - though check the insurance arrangements first.

Working from home

Though many new therapists set up at home, this can be very lonely, and in some cases, risky. It is usually better to start working at a natural health centre or well-run community centre (or even at your own training centre). Even if you clearly advertise 'Osteopathy for sports injuries' you will still get callers (especially if you are a woman) wanting hand relief massage. You will save money on room rent, of course. However, is your home suitable for seeing clients? Some of the factors to consider are who else is in the building, whether it is quiet and peaceful, whether there are enough loos, whether neighbours are discreet or interfering, and what other members of your household need. Working at home depends on whether you have a supportive partner (if you have a partner, that is) and whether your children (if you have them) understand what your work is about. Also consider the fact that there will be no casual callers as with a centre, so your client referrals will initially come from advertising, then through personal recommendation, and this may be a slow process. It's also hard to get away from work. The atmosphere from your clients can linger and you can be reminded of them by the surrounding artifacts.

You will be the only staff member: no one else to sort out the post, open the door if clients call at the wrong time; no sign outside advertising what you do (unless yours is a licensed clinic); no other practitioners around if you run out of essence. However, you can nibble at will, keep all your books and tools and equipment in the same place, and go for a snooze, peel the spuds, or pop the washing in the machine (or indeed write books) between clients.

Many practitioners, especially those established for some years, have worked successfully from home because they had no choice - there weren't any natural health centres in those days! Many of them describe themselves in directories as 'centres', and it is quite a surprise to find that a famous 'centre' is someone's second floor flat in a residential street. Some country therapists have gorgeous Swedish pre-fabricated wooden houses, and I know a suburban therapist who works, famously, from a squat.

You may of course be in the fortunate position of having exactly the right sort of home in the right locality and with a perfect little room than can he converted to a therapy room. If not, and you are currently hunting about for the right sort of place, avoid the residential lists and see if there are any vacated doctors' or dentists' surgeries available. There will already be at least one practice room, separated from the rest of the house and probably with its own telephone line, and the planning permission will already have been organised by the previous occupant.

The first time I consulted a now famous 'media' astrologer, he was working from a tiny bedsit above a shop; you had to enter up the back stairs from the rubbishy back yard, and the bath was under the stairwell. Healers, psychics, palmists and mediums tend to work from home, and so, of course do most psychotherapists.

If you work at home you will most certainly need an answering machine, and if you have a mobile phone, don't forget to switch it off during sessions or have one with a message-taking facility. Even if you don't work from home you will need and answer machine to refer callers to whichever centre you are working at on that day, and if you want to be super-efficient you will need a bleeper. There are other extras you can pay for such as call referral (if you work out of town sometimes). Certain of these services are only available for business lines, and in any case, it is probably worth having two phone lines - one for you, one for your practice. You may be willing for all the world to have your telephone number, but if you don't want everyone to have your address, rent a Post Office box number. The cost of these is very reasonable, and you can either collect mail at the sorting office, or arrange (for an additional fee) to have it delivered. These measures ensure privacy during dinner, your bath, or Cagney and Lacey.

Health centres and gyms

There are reflexologists working in city gyms and health clubs. Massage is offered in most saunas, and muscle-bound body-builders are not averse to a little yoga after a workout. If there are no natural health centres in your area you may decide that the local gym is better than working at home. There are also gyms and fitness centres in many large hotels. Most of these employ qualified sports teachers, and are therefore likely to be open to suggestions from you for activities or treatment that their residents or holiday-makers would enjoy on a rainy day. Don't forget local council leisure centres.

Have couch, will travel

Last, but becoming increasingly popular, is the travelling therapist who trucks about with a portable treatment couch, a case of oils, a car full of cushions and drawing materials, or a set of acupuncture needles. It is profitable to be able to offer a 'home service' as you can charge for your travelling time. I would have thought it was also necessary to have a reliable way of screening your clients, a portable telephone and a contact who always knows where you are supposed to be.

If the mobile life appeals, try getting yourself some business contacts, and offering a 'clinic' one day a week. Trade magazines such as *Health and Safety At Work* will give you a good idea of which companies are open to visiting therapists or have employee assistance programmes.

Just as country therapists work one or two days in the nearest town's health centre, therapists from cities also spend one or two days a week in 'commuter' towns - and charge city rates. A way to introduce yourself to the populace is to hold some weekend workshops in the area, or contact other therapists to see what the demand is like. If you can form a relationship with the local natural health centre (if there is one), this is obviously valuable; if not, there are GPs, adult education centres, libraries and similar places to leave your cards.

Once you have decided what you want, you can work out how to attract the clients. (You see how it always boils down to what you want.)

Issues Involved in Using Centres

Clients often use more than one practitioner in a centre, and this makes things difficult if they prefer your approach to another practitioner who is a personal friend or valued colleague - or of course, one of your own clients. I know at least one centre where this eventuality has been addressed directly by setting up small groups of practitioners who offer complementary services to clients.

From the point of view of a counsellor, if you find that the centre staff start to look on you as their personal agony aunty, or book appointments with you for all their friends, it is time to go. Believe it or not, counsellors and psychotherapists are still viewed with awe, and once it is revealed that they are human beings too, the disillusionment in their admirers can backfire disastrously. The staff, of course, listen to problems much of the time, for example when they are taking phone bookings. If they have no personal support it is inevitable that they will be storing up a lot of stuff they want to get rid of on the most likely person. Body practitioners have experienced being asked for 'a quick shoulder rub', or for advice on what remedy to give someone's partner or child, or any other sort of free advice. This is fine for a while, though it can become wearing, especially if there is no reciprocation of care or information.

Some centres pre-empt such problems and create codes of practice for everyone, so that all the people involved know where their responsibilities lie. With the best of intentions, boundaries can become very confused when the community ideal is that we are all equal.

This is another occasion where it is important to be clear both to whoever takes bookings, and to your clients, what is and what is not appropriate. Your client/volunteer may be taking bookings for new clients coming to see you, or meeting them in reception. This can be very damaging to the therapist-client relationship (which is an essential part of the therapy) and cause all sorts of repercussions. So if you are in a centre of this sort, you may need to find another source of clients. The scenario is even more complex if you are seeing the partner of a staff member or management committee member. Most psychotherapists will not see two clients who know each other socially. So your 'client net' has to be spread quite widely to avoid overlaps of this sort. Guidance is available from most professional associations and some training courses on sensible working practices in communities. For natural medicine practitioners, on the other hand, an important source of new clients will be friends of existing or past clients.

The therapy world is surprisingly small and peculiar examples of cosmic synchronicity crop up all the time, even in London, which you would think would be too big for such things to happen. They do!

There are several advantages of working in centres, so it is worth anticipating potential problems and having contingency plans for them. Information pouring into the letter box every day, and perhaps there is a library. As many natural health centres were originally set up by professional therapists, problems about boundaries and confidentiality may have been addressed from the start. If you have special needs, your colleagues will be willing to hear you.

So if you decide to work in a centre, and you select it carefully (assuming you have a choice) you should be fine. At least, if there are any problems, you will feel comfortable about expressing what's wrong and know that something will be done. If there isn't a suitable centre in your area, you could always start your own. One drawback of working in other people's rooms is that you can't stamp your own character on them. If you do work in other people's rooms you need to know you'll be allowed to move things around, or bring in your own lamps or mats or cushions, a favourite mug. Do ask if there is anywhere for you to store your information files, drawing materials, client files and similar, otherwise you will be trotting back and forth with these every day. If you keep client medical and treatment records, these should be accessible by no-one but you.

Another point to check in busy centres is whether you are booked in back-to-back with other practitioners. You need time before and after sessions and there are plenty of occasions where you need to go on for an extra few minutes. This may mean negotiating for extra time or probably paying for it, and it is well worth doing this.

I have had some excellent experience in one community centre and a ghastly experience in another, and on the whole better experiences in natural health centres. I would prefer to work at home, though being a sociable type I like to have other practitioners around. I enjoy the opportunity for shared information, shared promotion, such as joint talks, networking, mutual referrals, and learning about other disciplines, and the fact that someone else is responsible for locking up and making sure there's enough loo paper. Practitioners I know who work in two or three places; at home, at a training centre and at a clinic, for instance, say they enjoy the variety and the support which balances out all the travelling they need to do.

One thing that surprises me a greatly is that few natural health centres are accessible for disabled people, nor do they have disabled toilets (both these are legal requirements for funded centres and all public buildings). Few have lifts. This rules out all potential clients who are in wheelchairs, or their friends or partners who may have some sort of disability. It also means that therapists with disabilities are unable to work in any of these centres. I feel this is something that needs to be attended to by centre managers and incoming practitioners.

Selecting the right locality

'Where you work' also means which locality you want to work in, and this has a great deal to do with the type of clients you are hoping to attract.

How To Get More Clients

To attract wealthy clients, you need to work in a wealthy residential area, or if you are in a rural area, the market town, with plenty of parking space around and a reasonable amount of privacy and quiet. Smart city centre consulting rooms have high rents, so you will need to charge higher fees, and direct your advertising at better-off clients. As you cannot assume that all your clients will drive cars, you will also need to be reasonably near public transport. If you only see working clients in the evenings, it is no good being up a dark gloomy alley or a sinister back street. And bear in mind, if you work at home and want to charge high fees - working people may want sessions before breakfast. Can you and everyone else in your household accommodate that?

If you live in a small town, you also need to consider whether you want to bump into your clients at the local Spar, annual Church fete or outside the school when you are collecting your children. A way round this is to advertise your services outside the area you live in.

Researching the area

When determing where your potential clients are located geographically, there are other factors to be considered, including the number of other similar practitioners in your area, the population, and the other facilities available.

Time and Money

Determine How Much Time You Can Spare for Work

In the bad old days, we lived to work. Now, hopefully, we work to live. Working in holistic therapy is, in any case, more of a lifestyle than a job, and it tends to evolve, sometimes apparently beyond our control. The more experienced you become, the more intuitively you work, the more faith you have in your abilities, and the more difficult it is to retain a structure in your life. You may have noticed that friends from the old days seem to have fallen away, and new friends appear, some of whom are only interested in you when they are telling you their troubles. Do you want to be on duty all the time?

Even if you are not providing a muscular shoulder or words of wisdom, you are being bombarded constantly with new and interesting people, you hear of new thoughts and philosophies that seem just right for you at this moment. One day at an exhibition makes you realise how little you know, and how much you are missing out on. (I'm willing to bet that many of the people who book cut-price 'sample' sessions of various therapies at holistic fairs are off-duty therapists).

'Time' does not simply mean when your alarm goes off or how many hours a day you work or how long your sessions are. It means lazing time, meditating time, growing time, being time, travelling time, sleeping time, eating time, planning time, nothing time and, most important, the amount of time you wish to spend working. In your life plan, do you have a cut-off date, when you will take a sabbatical, go round the world, have more children, go and live in a community, write a book, set up your own centre, retire? The holistic business has not been going on long enough for people to work out when is a good time to stop. Pilots, police officers and various other workers are told firmly when to retire. Social workers, for instance, start to worry about burn-out after five years. Music industry executives know that their 'ears' go shortly after the age of 30 (this doesn't apply to George Martin). Not all of us want to be (or could be) Sir George Trevelyan. Mediums and channels seem to start their work quite late in life and many live to be 80 or more. A striking fact about many members of the holistic professions is their advanced age (especially psychotherapists). We therefore need to face the fact that our energy levels and self-renewing abilities are going to decrease as our interest, experience, abilities and spiritual strength increase.

It seems, therefore, wise to give serious thought to how many years you wish to spend actively practising therapy, and when would be the right time to start plugging in to something less demanding. Psychotherapists make commitments (or contracts) which require them to see someone for two or more years, once or more often per week, preferably at the same time. This may be early in the morning or after office hours, and obviously the demands on your time may change during that two years.

Getting more clients also has to mean earning enough money to make the most of tax concessions on pension plans for the self-employed.

If we hold the view that being a whole person is about the quality of life, this must also mean the quality of our entire lives, not just the working parts. What do you want to be doing when you are 60? 80? 101?Have another look at your life plan. A few years of intense activity, seeing ten clients a day plus groups, workshops, books, videos, teaching, supervision and whatever else I have forgotten, no holidays, creating your own philosophy and setting up your own training school or centre may be the best plan for you. Maybe you enjoy filling up your diary, maybe you get re-energised by watching other people growing and learning and progressing. That's fine - but will it always be the case? Isn't there a teeny little part of you saying - what about when I can't manage to work at this pace any more - then what?Allow a moment or two to plan for the 'then what?'. In other words, allow time for you.

If you need a lot of time for yourself, and have little energy to take on extra clients, you need to find other ways of earning money. Here are some ideas.If you want to work for the same amount of time and earn more money, and you do one-to-one work, then change over to couple or family therapy, groups or training. If organising workshops takes up more time than they are worth, then sign yourself up (for less money of course) with someone who does nothing but organise workshops, advertises them, and rakes in the clients for you. Or talk to some like-minded friend and set up a workshop team, rotating through the year. If thinking up workshops ideas isn't your strong point, you can probably create a three-year career with one single workshop by writing a best-selling book (and if attendance flags, you can tape the workshops and then sell the tapes).

There are numerous ways of organising your time. All you need to do is decide how much time you want to spend working (and by 'work' I include work-related activities, such as study and supervision and recovery time - all this is *other people's time.*) It is worth moving to a smaller house if it enables you to work shorter hours. Can you save on travelling time? (Perhaps this is why so many therapists work from home).

If you believe that 'time is money' then you will be reading this chapter with growing disbelief. The thing is, money comes and goes, time simply goes - you can never get it back. If you are earning a great deal of money, and have little time for yourself, look at whether you really need all that money.

Of course people's definitions of what 'work' actually is vary considerably. If you enjoy your work so much, and your whole life revolves around it, then you are 'giving time to yourself'. On the other hand, if work is only about earning money, then you are not. Outside the holistic world, people's identities are still very much associated with what they do; here, I hope, people are more concerned with who they are.

What Are Your Energy Levels?

The type of energy you have is your biggest asset. Can you define yours? Is it physical, mental, emotional, spiritual? Do you know where it comes from, goes to, and how it can be restored? When you are physically exhausted, what keeps you going - bright ideas? Love? A snooze? A good read? Food? When you are emotionally drained, what nourishes you? Are you aware of when you are spiritually or emotionally drained? Do you recognise your own stress signals?

Physical energy is usually the easiest to determine, as it is about strength, stamina, good health and fitness. That said, there are therapists who are out of touch with their bodies, especially those who work intuitively or with the arts, or who react emotionally to physical stress (and vice versa). *Mental energy* is also relatively obvious: if you 'can't think straight' or have 'run out of ideas' you undoubtedly know this.

Emotional energy is not such an easy one to spot - feeling 'depressed' can have numerous causes. If you feel physically well and are not tired and wonder why you are miserable, possibly you are feeling unloved; if you are otherwise fit and lively but ache inside, you may be in emotional pain. On the other hand, if you develop abdominal pains or palpitations, it may be because you are unhappy.

Psychic or spiritual energy is the hardest to identify (except for those people who work purely with this); it is at its lowest when you are doing too much (healer-depletion) or when you are under psychic attack or being zapped.

If you have not experienced psychic attack, it feels as if someone (unconsciously or not) hates you with such intensity that it seems their life depends on maintaining this hate, and watching you trip over yourself, fail at whatever you do, and feel constantly exhausted. Their 'hate' has rarely anything to do with you personally, and you can learn to protect yourself once you know you are being zapped and who is doing it. It is also possible to enable the person (if it's someone you need to be close to) to express and discharge their hate, or at least to acknowledge the shadow side of themselves. Here is an example of psychic attack. While I was writing this paragraph, I was thinking of two people who, at various times in my life, have for reasons only they know zapped me in this way. As I tried to explain the sensation, the screen of this computer began to flicker, and within moments, a message flashed up telling me there was a system fault. I had to switch off, wait, and start all over again. I found this page and, of course, what I had written had disappeared into the bowels of the computer. I also feel moved to add that these two people - both healers - believe that they are saints; in addition, they use their healing abilities to attempt to control people, and demand a great deal of attention.

Looking on the bright side (!) loss of psychic energy can simply mean that you are doing too much, giving out too much, not protecting yourself before sessions and forgetting to 'cleanse' after sessions. This is most commonly experienced by new practitioners, who are working hard to build up their client lists and don't want to turn anyone down. They may also have huge loans to repay, so they can't afford to take time off for themselves. A sudden loss of psychic energy can be extremely dangerous - so if you pick up signals, do take a rest. It's really not worth pushing yourself. I know someone who actually fell flat on her face in the middle of a conversation with friends, struck down, as it were.

Fortunately most of us have more than one reliable energy source so that we can use one when the other is depleted, and it's important to know how you balance out before you start building up your list. Physical energy is obviously more important for body therapists, and being low in energy of one sort or another is not always a bad thing; some therapists work well when they are feeling sad - it can make them more empathic or compassionate (hopefully for themselves as well, as long as their boundaries are intact). However, deep emotional pain makes it impossible to work at any giving level.

It is possible to work in an intellectual or intuitive way when you are physically tired. When you are feeling thick-headed, it is often physical activity which clears your mind. If you listen all day you can become mentally clogged, and it might be good to get a massage, say. The most reviving for 'listeners' is to talk to someone, and if you don't have a supervisor or similar support worker, and no one wants to be talked at, go and give a talk, or write one into your work schedule.If this becomes urgent ring a radio phone-in programme and complain about something.

Energy never goes away, it merely goes elsewhere, or gets stuck in a part of you. You have physical, emotional, mental and spiritual boundaries. If you know where they are you can apply them. If you don't say 'stop' your body will say it for you (as we keep telling our clients).

If you can identify the one aspect of your energy that will never let you down, put this at the top of your list of personal assets. Human beings (as I keep saying) are extraordinary. Look at the example of Stephen Hawking, Professor of Cosmology at Cambridge, famous for having a phenomenal brain and almost discovering the secret of the Universe despite spending the last 20 years or more dying slowly of Motor Neurone Disease - just one example of the staggering powers of the human spirit.

Establishing a Support Network

Supervision, as I have mentioned elsewhere, is something that no psychotherapist would want to be without. Many other holistic practitioners have some kind of formal professional support, and it is generally accepted that we all need five people in our lives; one of whom may be a professional (supervisor or therapist) and the others supportive friends/partner/colleague. At least one of your team should be in the same line of work as you are. People who have not been working for long enough to identify their support needs, or have yet to find their five people, could find that being on courses, or attending workshops, gives them the input and contacts that they need. You may find that you achieve the same results by switching off from people altogether; slumping in front of the telly, reading poetry, wandering along the seashore. However, as I shall keep repeating, we are in a people business, though in saying this I am by no means ignoring animal homeopaths or those who package vegetarian pet foods.

Before taking on new clients, look at the support network that you have now. Admitting that you are needy and vulnerable is difficult when your clients all think you are strong and powerful. This may of course be true, in terms of your *work* - but what about your human needs? If you often feel bored, angry, tired, or worried, and there are no obvious external stressors, then you are not receiving enough support. You may have ways of closing down after work, of cleansing your aura, of centering yourself - perhaps by a form of meditation, subtle breaths, Tai Chi or yoga. Perhaps you shower and go jogging or dancing. You probably know how to cleanse your practice room. All this is about shaking off the junk that you pick up during the working day. There is still you, the needy little you, who requires attention.

If you do not have five people, nor even a supportive partner, then you need to give yourself much more time to unwind, play, centre yourself, and relax. I don't believe that anyone except a few genuine gurus is so self-sufficient that they do not need the company of other human beings, or the occasional shoulder to cry on. Many practitioners (especially women) believe that they *have* to cope. They say 'I can't cope' and then they pull themselves together and do cope, when there is no reason at all why they should not simply give in, not cope, and cancel everything for the day (or week). Life's hard, why should we be expected to cope with it simply because we are therapists? In addition, if you never allow yourself to feel depressed, de-skilled, depleted or resentful, how can you empathise with clients who express such feelings? And, more to the point, how can you be there for them next week?

There are short courses on how to avoid burn-out, and, looking at it more positively, there are thousands of ways to enjoy life that don't cost you any money. Whatever you do, you will need to do more of it if you take on more clients. Allow ample time for this in your working week, otherwise you will wish you had kept things as they were.

If you identify with the 'wounded healer' concept then, unless you have worked through all your own wounds, they are going to be constantly jabbed at by your clients/group members/students. I have been on workshops where the leader was all over the place, and on more than one where the clients ended up taking care of things. Very empowering for us, of course, but not what we had paid our money for. In each case, the workshop leader believed he/she was above all that, and a guru besides. Apart from needing professional slaps on the wrist, these people also clearly needed considerable personal support, and were not receiving enough of it. At the very minimum, you need some sort of constant way of checking whether your boundaries are intact. Psychotherapy is said to be 'acceptable co-dependance'. I'm not sure I go along with that; even if it is true, it does not mean that the state of co-dependence should continue outside the therapy room.

Identify where you need personal support or professional support. Professional support, of course, has to be paid for - personal support does not always (well, not with money, at least).

How Much Money Do You Want?

People part with money when they want to buy something. Therapy is one of the things that they can buy, so you are selling it to them. For some therapists, it may require a leap of the imagination to perceive 'selling' a therapy or service as if it was a product. However, it is. And if you are going to be realistic about earning a living, you need to be aware that money is a medium of exchange and not (necessarily) the root of all evil. People pay you to work and therapy is work (often extremely hard work) therefore it is worth someone's money.

Another thing about money is that the 'pool' available to us all is, like energy, always there. It moves around, gets exchanged, goes up and down and in an out, sometimes gets wasted or thrown around, and sometimes drips gently down upon us (the Biblical Manna may indeed have been the fabled Pennies from Heaven). All you need to do is be standing in the right place with your hat upside down and believe that your turn will come.

If you don't like to think of money, think of lubricants, or energy, or the tides or even the stars. Astrologically speaking, if your money aspect is linked to Saturn you will only be rich every 29 years, of course. Or if it is linked to the Moon (as it is for most people) you'll be paid monthly. Look back and see if you can find out what your money is linked to, what you have been paid the most for. (It may well have been something you didn't *like*, of course, which is why you are now a holistic therapist.) However, your skill and knowledge which convinced some-one to pay you, perhaps over the odds, *is still with you,* and can be applied to your new work.

If you have done a business plan you may already know where the most reliable source of income in your field will come from. Earning more money does not always mean getting more clients. You could, for instance, increase your fees, change your advertising 'pitch' in order to reach better-paid clients, or change your style of working in order to do the same. If you just want regular money with no hassles, then consider working with other professionals only.

The psychotherapy world in particular is noted for being somewhat self-supporting: all trainees have to be in therapy throughout their course (at least four years) and usually want to stay in therapy longer than that; all working psychotherapists need lifelong supervision, and to continue their professional development in other ways (training in different styles of practice, or learning new methods). Supervisors have to have supervision too. This may sound incestuous, however, as long as everyone is clear about their boundaries, and therapists don't attend workshops where their clients or their supervisors are likely to be, things seem to work out OK.

It may not be regular money that draws you to working with your colleagues, of course - it may be that you have a talent for it and enjoy it. It is conceivable that these types of formal arrangements may become *de rigeur* in other areas of holistic practice in due course. So why not start now?

If you want to make more money and see more clients, then you may feel that doing one-to-one work, plus groups/workshops, plus training, plus writing articles would be a good idea. However, there is an argument that seeing ten clients a day for five days a week will bring you more money for far less risk and effort than seeing fewer clients, and running courses and workshops. The additional energy required in advance planning, preparation and re-building your energy afterwards can actually work out more costly. If you know that after a workshop you need a massage and a float, this has to be built into your workshop budget along with all the other costs. A knowledge of what drains you, and what energises you, will help you make this decision; if there's not much in it, a few quick sums will tell you which is more cost-effective for you. If you don't want to employ yourself for the whole week, you could offer yourself to a college or adult education centre. Some of these are increasingly offering courses on holistic therapies, especially in cities. The pay is small, but you have a guaranteed basic income for about 40 weeks of the year.

You may want all your different ventures to be inter-connected, and working towards the same central target - which is getting more clients, or earning more money (which ever way you see it). If so, you will be working in a buoyant cross-referral system: a book will attract clients to the workshop-of-the-book and vice versa; talks and workshops will bring you in more clients, people you see for individual therapy will want to come to your workshops. If this makes your boundaries start to look a bit too elastic, then consider taking the opposite route: do certain types of work with one set of people and other types of work with other sets, altering your targets (and therefore your publicity and marketing) accordingly. You could even have different names for different areas of your practice.

Only you can decide how much money you want - which is not the same as how much money you need. Be aware that different members of our community have different attitudes towards paying you, and very different ways of valuing what you do for a living. Some actually resent people who appear to be 'making money' - usually those who have never been self-employed, or who work in community/voluntary/social work jobs.

If you want a lot of money, big business is where it is. If you want to be rich and famous, then aim at being on TV, on the radio, and written about in the national press. To do this you will need immense chutzpah, a speciality (you can only do one thing) and a team of other professionals such as a manager, and agent, a publicist, a lawyer, an accountant, and a secretary (known, in Hollywood, as your 'people'). Also you will have to very good at another thing - acting. One of the drawbacks of deciding to specialise is that as you grow yourself, you move on past the very thing that you are teaching others. If you have become world famous for your assertion training, which teaches people how to stand up to rude waiters, you have some teeth-gritting years ahead of you as you yearn to work with people a little more assertive and challenging than the ones who flock to your world famous seminars.

For further suggestions, see How To Become Obscenely Wealthy.

What is Money?

If you are reading this book because you want to make money, rather than get more clients, and you haven't had a prior career as a currency broker, you need to understand how money works so that you can get rich.

Borrowing money

This is necessary if you haven't any money to start with. In this country we have a really bizarre money system which, it must be said, is designed to keep the rich rich and the rest of us in our place. Cynical stockbrokers will tell you that as soon as the 'Mums and Dad' start buying shares, they immediately sell theirs. What do they know that the 'Mums and Dad' don't know?

First, the system is designed so that you can't get hold of any of this money unless you stay in the system. Even exploiting the masses means you are staying in the system, as you will be selling your wares to people who believe in the system. Money has to be thought of (when you are borrowing it) as 'seed'. In fact, several banks refer to their start-up loans to small business as 'seed money' - it makes them feel they are doing something natural and wholesome. You also have to pay them a fee for the honour of them lending you money.

Unfortunately money is actually designed to disempower you, as it keeps you in debt to the lender and therefore in their power. You can never get out of debt because though you may seem rich on paper, the value of this paper fluctuates to such an extent that every so often there is a 'crash', and now and then colossal frauds are perpetrated in order to raise money from one source to pay off a debt to another. The banks (for instance) have the money, and they 'sell' it to you very expensively by charging you 'interest' in what they sell you (this is called Lending). However, it is not even their money that they are lending you - it's their depositors'. There is a moral in that old coconut 'Never a lender nor a borrower be'. While you are using your 'loan' as capital for your project or new business, you earn some money. This is not, of course, *your* money yet (as you owe it to the bank); however, you will still have to pay tax on what you earn - you only get tax relief on the interest you pay, not the original capital sum. So you lose out twice.

The point of all this is to keep you in the system, which, incidentally, means that however rich you become, you remain in Stage 2 or 3. People who set themselves up in business to make a lot of money frequently become money brokers, or, occasionally, Lloyds Underwriters (and we all know what happens to them in a bad year). However the people who circulate the money packages among such idiots make a fortune. So do the brokers who make a living out of selling you insurance policies, pension plans, investment trusts, and the various other forms of money 'packages'. They even refer to new schemes to make money out of you as 'products', and give themselves awards, such as 'Best Designed New Product', in order to make them seem artistic, respectable and nice. This proves that they think of a lump of money as a Thing to be sold, not as pounds and pence at all.

I hope it is becoming clear that this system has nothing whatsoever to do with the holistic way of life. The best you can do is to try and borrow money from one of the 'green' money companies, and if you are fortunate enough to have money to invest, please invest it in one of these companies. You will receive a lower rate of interest, however, it will mean other practitioner and holistic business people can therefore borrow it at a lower rate of interest.

So, going back to the idea of money as 'seed', there is no point borrowing any unless you have green fingers. Money is, basically, legalised co-dependence, and all the real values of it disappear because there is such an obvious power imbalance.

How to become obscenely wealthy

This list is for those who only want money and are not interested in anything else in life. Since I need to earn a living, and therefore sell more books, I know that people who want to make money often buy books which tell them how to do it. This list is for them.

1) Being an aristocrat and inheriting £300 million because a 14th century ancestor won a battle and the King who awarded the land and property said it had to be hereditary and therefore bought all the descendants' loyalty in perpetuity.
2) Being a criminal
3) Being a multi-media mega mogul.
4) Writing, producing, directing and starring in five different version of the same film which appeals to Stage 3 people who like competitiveness and winning.

OR

Writing and directing five versions of the same film which include every possibly fairy tale and myth, set in the future, and preferably perpetuating the erroneous belief that there is a battle between Good and Evil.
5) Being hugely talented and creating numerous international hit stage musicals
6) Pretending you know the secret of eternal life (e.g. by founding a religion)
7) Selling the real secret of life
8) Manufacturing a socially-acceptable addictive chemical substance which makes its consumers dependant on you
9) Being a dictator.

If none of the above appeal, there are plenty of other ways of earning a living. The quickest and easiest way is by trading on the misfortunes of others - buying up stock from bankrupt firms extremely cheaply and selling it at slightly more. Another way is to put an ad in the paper saying 'Make Thousands Instantly - tiny initial outlay. Send £25 for instruction pack.' Then you send responders an 'instruction pack' which tells them to do exactly what you did.

An even quicker way is to produce something very cheap which appeals to people's most basic instincts as there is only one thing which unites us all and that is the Individual Survival instinct. If you are a baker you can make a lot of money by saying there is a bread shortage because everyone will rush out and stockpile. A more holistic way is to say the local water is poisoned, and sell everyone water filters. (Incidentally Individual Survival is not the same thing as the Secret of Life). The type of products which will sell in this category are all forms of self-protection, self-presentation and feeling good, such as weapons, Kung Fu courses, fast food, pain-killers, good-luck charms, insurance policies, burglar alarms, smoke detectors, 'eternity' pills, pension schemes, condoms, and for that matter absolutely anything at all to do with sex, including motorbikes.

A little of the above cynicism - or rather realism - would help charities raise funds quicker than all those heart-rending photographs appealing to our generosity and begging for donations. The Terrence Higgins Trust will probably make more money from its explicit safe sex video for gay men than from all the fund-raising appeals of the previous year. I suspect that a charity involved in famine relief could do very well out of a survival diet book, though they may feel shy about marketing it.

Hundreds of holistic entrepreneurs - spearheaded by astrologers - make an excellent living out of telephone services. Even the internationally celebrated psychic Vasso is not above having a dial-a-prediction line. These services pay well and have to, as you need to advertise them in national newspapers almost every day. They are also frequently deceptive. Though you might hear the celebrated seer's voice on tape, it is unlikely that he or she will have had the time to write their own scripts or do their own forecasts. Holistic hacks around the country make a reasonable living producing these 'readings'. Ah well. Nothing is a what it appears to be.

The reality of money-making is that people are more interested in survival than in anything else. So if you are also selling the evidence for life after death, you can't really go wrong, can you?

I am always truly in awe at the inventiveness of people who want to make money and are too twee to say so. They come up with truly wonderful ways of disguising their motives - Tantric Sex was a good one, though I don't think many people were taken in and it hasn't done that well. There is also something a bizarre and unpleasant about the selling to white men the ancient manhood rituals of Native American Indians, bearing in mind that these became known only because other white men massacred most of them, annexed their lands, ghettoised the survivors and stole their secrets (and, about 500 years ago, all their treasures and icons).

Herein lies a moral: be extremely careful if you really do know the secret of life, because someone will try extremely hard to steal it from you. Cannibals used to eat the flesh of their dead enemies out of respect and in an attempt to gain some of their strength. Oddly there are still people who believe that if they can control you, they will automatically discover your secret. As we all know, this does not actually work, because you can never use someone else's secret because it won't work for you.

This is the *real* secret, and this is what you are really marketing - the way for individuals to discover their individual secret of life. This book is one of those ways.

You won't become obscenely rich doing one-to-one therapy. In fact you won't become moderately rich. Here are some ways to become moderately rich, which hopefully may lead on to further wealth.

• Set up a training course and charge high fees. Offer franchises.
• Organise supervision courses for trainers.
• Write a book, or better still, a series of books on a speciality and run courses based on the books. Don't forget the extra revenue from audio and video tapes.
• Buy and sell products related to the therapy e.g. aromatherapy oils.
• Organise people around you who are willing to promote you. Make sure they have skills in dealing with the media.
• Watch out for that trend and fill the need with a speciality only you can offer.
• Organise large group events where you are the star. For instance lectures or workshops where you can net a crowd of people. Big groups means big bucks.
• Create a movement (see section following shortly).

However, money isn't everything, which leads us to the next subject.

Building a Career

When considering ways of building your career, think of lateral ways of growing, not just vertical ways. This is especially the case if you are self-employed. You need to keep an eye open for business opportunities. Listen to what clients ask for. What are their needs? How can you satisfy them? If they keep asking you about a particular book, why not stock it? You could order it from the publisher or distributor direct with a discount of 35%. If they constantly ask you about relaxation tapes or music tapes, then stock them. If you find some of them want a particular kind of training then consider setting up a training to meet this need. Of the ten practitioners I know most closely, all of them are working in ways other than one-to-one therapy. I know two osteopaths who, with a homeopath, have set up their own natural health clinic; two aromatherapists (one of whom is also a counsellor) who import and market their own oils. One of them also started an aromatherapy training school and later opened her own holistic health centre. One of the counsellors I know teaches, runs groups, supervises students, runs workshop series here and abroad, teaches batik, and has just spent five weeks in the U.S. on a further training course.

Of course the best way to assure yourself of a lifelong career in psychotherapy is to be an analyst. You see clients three or four times a week, can charge outrageous fees because BUPA will pay them (assuming your clients are members), and the medical profession believe in you. Even better, all students of analytical psychotherapy have to have about five years of analysis themselves, and so it goes on, an endless self-perptuating myth.

Back to reality. I know a clinical psychologist who joined a religious group while abroad and later set up a London centre for study, retreats, meditation, workshops, and selling books about the faith. Then he started his own psychotherapy training school and still sees individual clients.

Another practitioner I know, (and I keep thinking of more as I write) is a psychotherapist, group facilitator, trainer, supervisor and lately 'media' therapist. She gets asked to appear on day-time TV programmes talking about aspects of therapy. She also teaches police and nurses about working with bereaved relatives, is about to set up her own centre, and is invited to hold weekend workshops on personal growth all around the UK.

One successful psychotherapist said to me 'I always look at what I am good at and what are the opportunities within this field.' It is also natural that those whose work purpose is to enable clients to realise and develop their true potential should also want to do this for themselves. Body practitioners tend to expand their practices physically. That is, they start to import massage tables, produce books, tapes or videos, create a range of oils or body lotions and similar practical products.

The New Age really exists, and I believe it began at the end of World War II. Having seen how incompetent people in authority could be, us ordinary folk started wondering whether there was another way, and discovered that we are perfectly capable of taking responsibility for ourselves. Then we met lots of people like us who wanted to learn and, as you've noticed, this desire for self-empowerment continues and will hopefully never abate. As would be expected, the demand for individual psychotherapy is changing. Few clients rely on one-to-one therapy only. They try natural therapies, join self-help groups, go to workshops, read books, and magazines, listen to tapes, go to fairs, take massage, Shiatsu and Tai Chi courses, and spend holidays in Devon or Greece or Arizona or Switzerland which are often one-week personal growth workshops. Practitioners of any discipline who have not noticed this change in demand may find themselves left behind.

Look for every opportunity to expand your practice and develop your talents. There are plenty out there. It's wise to act quickly, as ideas circulate freely and someone somewhere is probably writing a book very like this one. Do not take my word for it. Aristotle (or perhaps Mrs. Aristotle) announced that the purpose of life was happiness; in terms of working for a living, Goethe (or maybe Goethe's Mum) said:

'Until one is committed, there is hesitancy, the chance to draw back, always ineffectiveness. Concerning all acts of initiative and creation, there is one elementary rule - the ignorance of which kills countless ideas and splendid plans; that the moment one definitely commits oneself, then Providence moves too. All sorts of things occur to help one that would never otherwise have occured. A whole stream of events issues from the decision, raising in one's favour all manner of unforeseen incidents and meetings and material assistance, which no (wo)man could have dreamed would have come his/her way.

'Whatever you can do or dream you can, begin it. Boldness has genius, power, and magic in it. Begin it now.'

As I feel uncomfortable with the notion that it's all down to providence, I like to interpret this philosophy as being observant enough to notice the opportunities, being aware of how your needs can be met, and having faith in yourself. Life has flung as much junk at me as the average person, however, I have noticed that as long as I feel like a victim, things get worse. As soon as I start looking for ways out of whichever hole I'm in, I notice what is going on out in the world and the world takes notice of me.

We all relate to the world in our preferred ways, rather like choosing the same type of clothes to wear all the same. This means we are not using ourselves to our fullest abilities. If you want to expand your practice, and perhaps team up with some colleagues, it is useful to take a team-building and personality test, such as the Myers-Briggs Type Indicator. This is based on Jungian psychology, (and designed with his help) and divides us into 16 basic groups on four scales, with two opposing preferences on each (such as extravert or introvert). These show where our attention is focussed and where we get our energy and ideas from, the way perceive events, the way we make decisions and the way we apply our knowledge and abilities to life.

You may know you are a leader, for instance, though if you have had no opportunity to prove it, you won't have much confidence in your abilities. According to the Myers-Briggs system, there are four types of successful managers, which can be roughly summarised as: (1) quiet, orderly, decisive, responsible administrators (2) purposeful, independent, original self-starters (3) frank, decisive, knowledgeable, active leaders and (4) practical, realistic, money- or mechanically-minded organizers.

If you are thinking of setting up a group practice, and you are all the same types of people, it will probably fail. Though most of us can turn our hands to anything we have to and often enjoy the learning process, it makes more sense to devote yourself to the work you do best, and let someone else handle the rest. You may be a reliable, loyal follower rather than a leader, or an all-rounder, resourceful but hopeless at administration. Some people work happily in a co-operative, others champ at the bit, wanting their partners to keep up with their visions. A very simple and quick assessment process can prevent countless problems in the future. Another helpful thing about such tests (done by the right practitioner) are that they also show you what is holding you back from success for an intuitive feeling type, it may well be loneliness, since you make up only 12% of the population. Other blocks to success are low self-worth, guilt, carrying or rescuing everybody, a desire to avoid any sort of conflict, 'unfinished business', especially old jealousies or resentment, or the need for a Knight in Shining Armour.

People who make wonderful practitioners - gentle, committed, friendly and patient - should team up with someone easy-going and accepting who knows how to assemble facts and make things happen. People who work on intuition, need plenty of time alone and are able to absorb themselves in work until they reach the end, need dependable, organised, thorough, financially-adept partners.

Without a good understanding of ourselves, we might soldier on, trying to run the wrong business or avoiding setting up the right one, because we don't know that we have the capabilities. As so many holistic practitioners work on intuition, and rely on their inner world for ideas, then having to be logical or analytical, will be quite difficult. Spontaneous people who like to keep their options open will not be too happy with forward planning. This does not mean that the required skills cannot be learned. Some of the best ideas flounder because their originators forgot about publicity, or they didn't have enough skills to put the ideas into practice.

That said, determination can make entrepreneurs of us all. So follow Goethe's advice, and whichever way you feel you can expand your practice, start doing it now. As practitioners, you have to be adaptable, sometimes minute by minute, to your clients. You can be as adaptable in your work. One of my favourite Somerset Maugham short stories is *The Verger*, about a man who got fired by the new vicar, because he couldn't read or write. Disconsolate, he wandered home along a dreary road, desperate for a cigarette. There wasn't a tobacconists in sight. With his savings, he started a shop there, did well, and gradually built a huge chain of shops, by dint of wandering about the suburbs looking for streets without tobacconists. Finally his bank manager asked him in, suggesting he invest some of his millions, and handed him some proposals to look it. The man blushed, and said he couldn't read or write, though he could count. Said the bank manager, 'Great heavens, - you're a rich man! Imagine what you would have achieved if you'd been able to read and write.'

'I can tell you that,' was the answer. 'I'd still be the verger at the Parish Church.'

What abilities can you bring from previous jobs?

People who discovered, in their 30s or 40s perhaps, that they had developed clairvoyance or healing abilities (the discovery which led to their new training) 'forget' all the earthly things which motivated them before - being sales rep of the year, buying a bigger house or seeing their name in print, or being allowed to use the executive loo, or owning their own taxi fleet. At the same time as 'forgetting' they devalue all the personal and professional skills that they learned and developed during their previous working lives. It is these people who are the most shocked to discover that holistic business can be as much of a rat race as any other and that commercial skills are needed. Much of what you learnt in your previous career may be very useful to you as a practitioner. Remind yourself of the skills you have from your previous work history and see if you can apply them to marketing your business. The similarities may not seem obvious at first, but you may be suprised if you look closely.

Just as every person has their own *intrinsic* value to us all, and all parts of nature are interdependent, every ability you have can be put to good use in your work, if not directly, then certainly in getting you more clients. If this idea seems puzzling at first, try identifying your skills in groups such as practical, intellectual, emotional and intuitive.

What was your most obvious previous work skill, the one by which you sold yourself at interviews? Being a self-starter? Organisational ability? Impressive speaker? Good teamworker? Your sensitivity and ability to empathise? Your position as Equal Opportunities rep? Your calmness under pressure? Your ability to think on your feet? Or to transfer your enthusiasm for your product to customers? Your pleasure in meeting new people which made you the first choice to staff the company stand at a fair? Your patience, reliability, perseverance, thoroughness? Your ability to translate briefs into works of art?

It is also helpful to be aware of what you cannot do, in which case you can team up with someone whose skills are complementary to yours. Don't worry if you know nothing about the finer points of advertising, publicity, exhibitions, administration, the psychology of colour, printing, mail-shots, the voluntary sector, or book publishing - someone else will.

Marketing essentials will be covered in Section II of this guide. You are a brilliant therapist, so there is no need to feel you have to be a brilliant marketeer. You are not out to conquer the world, you just want to get a few more clients. You don't need to be able to do everything by yourself. If you are not artistic, and you do not want artistic clients, there is no need to attempt to produce an artistic brochure. If you are extremely artistic, you may prefer not to produce a brochure at all, but something quite out of the ordinary.

I knew a man who wanted a job producing the scripts for the 'prompter' devices - called auto-cues - that TV newscasters read when you think they are looking straight at you. He built a small model TV and rolled his CV round a tube with knobs either end, tucked it inside, and got the job.

The point of this anecdote is that this man's previous job was in child care, and he spent most of the day teaching the children how to make toys with various cast-offs from their parents. So you never know what previous work talents can be applied to your new career.

Such things are vastly expensive to produce for the mass market. However, if you only want 12 people at your workshop you need only produce 20 or 30 special 'brochures' to send to enquires. If you were once a lollipop lady, you could make little lollipops to send to the little people you are going to kindly lead safely across the Great Divide. I will go into this in more detail in the chapter on leaflets.

How to create a movement

A 'movement' can be described as a form of therapy which comes across as new, is readily explained, and captures the public imagination, because it is *just what was needed.*

Some examples of movements are: yoga, TM, aromatherapy, recovery, co-dependence, mythology, Native American philosophy, men's groups, Shiatsu, veganism, and self-help.There are hundreds more. How many of them are genuinely new? How did the original practitioners who brought these movements to the public attention know they would be so popular? Either they had perfect intuition or they did their homework.

To be successful for many years to come, you have to plan to be there with what is needed when the need arises. It's obviously futile to do something that someone else did ten years ago successfully, because the market you are working towards will not be the same at all.

Every industry in the world has researchers who collect data in order to predict trends and produce the goods that consumers will want next year, and the year after. Businesses which do not do this go broke. The same rules apply to holistic practitioners - so if you cannot think up (or intuit) a 'movement', or do not want to, find out how to be one step ahead of the rest.

To become successful, or even famous, you cannot do the same thing as everyone else, even if you are the most brilliant of all practitioners in your field. This only works in allopathic medicine, where the most revered and highest paid specialist is the one who knows the most about the disease (or 'syndrome', named after him/her) which affects the least number of people.

A practitioner who keeps an eye on current affairs, societal changes, reads a little history and does a little research, can predict what will be needed ten years from now, if only a different name for an old therapy. Just as it is pointless buying a house at the peak of a property boom, it is pointless changing your therapy to something that is currently hugely popular. For example, if every aromatherapist you know has a six-month waiting list, don't merely study aromatherapy - set up a training centre and a professional association. Better still, start courses to train aromatherapy teachers. Look for all the possibilities in your own field first.

Remember that all new products and services create their own sub-industries.

Think about how the holistic business has developed and how it is now a complete industry, or rather community, with its own publications, magazines and directories, libraries, modes of operation, training systems, course recognition systems, professional associations, networks, accreditation, regulations, licensing, jargon, educational literature, colleges, print print and more print, mail-order companies, book publishers, writers, its own visual identity (sort of) its heroes and heroines, its codes of behaviour (unspoken) its self-regulating methods, its own computer programmes, its own music and poetry, its ways of assessing people, a certain style for centres, fairs; its ways of recognising each other - clothes, image, crystals, food preferences, water filters, barefoot boogies; its own holiday resorts, even radio stations. It's a microcosm of life. It has links with other communities, too, such as such as the 'green' movement, the peace movement, and is, of course international.

As soon as you detect a new trend, look ahead. What needs will this new trend create? How can you be the first to supply what is needed? Think 'Army'. One day someone thought it would be a good idea to have an army. Then they realised that they would have to have uniforms, barracks, weapons, ammunition and transport. They would need food, catering staff, laundries, horses, feed for the horses, stables, vets, training for the recruits, communications, ways of telling people how to join the army, experts in every possible craft and trade to provide training for people to teach the soldiers how to do all the different types of work required, secret codes and signalling systems, map-makers, doctors and nurses, hospitals, schools, crockery, cutlery, pay-roll systems, courts and jails and lawyers and military police, sports and leisure activities, a postal service, and thousands of other things necessary to create a completely self-sufficient community.They would also need land to build camps on, its own special jargon, a hierarchical structure, ways of predicting the weather, and lots and lots of money to pay for all this. Though the army may be a totally non-holistic example, the same build-up applies to every other industry. All of them become 'communities'. One tiny new product requires a huge set of back-up systems such as packaging, marketing, research, advertising, manufacturing, testing, distribution, raw materials, workers, executives, trade and consumer publications, fairs, and so on.

To be alert to potential opportunities for a career expansion, you need only to be an observer of your own environment and understand the relevance of important social and lifestyle changes. For example, in the last ten years word processors have become a major tool in the corporate world, breeding a generation of operators glued to a VDU screen. Opertors of these machines complain of stiff necks, shoulders and arms. Some massage schools have now penetrated this market and go to the offices where these operators work and give massage sessions. What a brilliant idea! Follow the trends and be aware of what people need. Then come up with an idea to meet this need.

One morning you may wake up and think 'I wish there was a...'. When this happens, go with your instinct, and invent or create whatever it is your unconscious knows is needed.

On a more practical level, knowledge of variations in the market is important. If you pitch your therapy at men under 26, you are working for a diminishing market. An observation of the divorce statistics (see below) might also indicate that family therapists are in for a rough time. Continuing populations require that couples who have children have on average 2.4 children. If they only have 1.4, the population is shrinking rapidly. Finnish people apparently have so few children that the race is practically dying out.

Look back into recent history and see which social trends led to the need for particular therapies. The stock market Big Bang produced a huge demand for fitness centres for young market makers; the Big Collapse created a huge stress management industry, plus career guidance and debt counselling. Can you work out why the boom of the early 90s was (and still is) the 'recovery industry'? Can you predict what therapies will be needed five, 10, 20 years from now?

This kind of 'actuarial' work does not require any special skills, just interest, the awareness that you need to know, the ability to collect information and make connections, and your own intuition. Any astrologer could have told you that the past 20 years would produce time-saving gadgets and massive improvements in communications. You don't have to be a visionary. Genius is (as we all know) only one per cent inspiration. History will help you. Feminists have for 25 years been predicting the collapse of the traditional family, and here we have it, 500-plus people a day filing for divorce (most of them women), and numerous members of the previously rock-solid (or perhaps long-suffering) Royal Family deciding that marriage is as hopeless an institution as the Monarchy.

Anyone who read anything about the proposals for the Single Market 20 years ago was able to predict that we would all have to be categorised and accredited and recognised. And what about the Chunnel,which appears to be an even greater threat to the British Identity than the Single Market - we have, after all, always been an island and haven't been invaded since 1066. This is a huge collective threat. I quite expect a whole new market in rabies-prevention crystals to be sold to people living around the entrance to the Channel Tunnel, for instance.

Someone will soon start a 'detox' centre in Central London, where for half an hour you can breathe pure clean air, drink special tisanes, be given homoeopathic remedies for carbon monoxide poisoning, and therapeutic lotions to rub on your face to heal the burst capillaries.

You do not have to be in touch with global changes to be successful (though it helps, especially if you want to create a movement). The most important thing is to be aware when what you are doing is *special.* I know an aromatherapist who mixed her own potions and perfumes and sold them to clients for specific conditions. Some of her clients, business women, saw their potential, and backed her in forming a company to bottle and market the potions. The thought would never have occured to her by herself, as she didn't think she was doing anything special, she just found it easier to work using her own mixtures.

The trend now as I have said, is for multi-people with widely-varied careers involving therapies and related products. And your clients don't have to be 'the public' - they can be other therapists. There are so many of us now that we have collectively created a completely new set of needs and requirements that didn't exist ten years ago. Here's one little example: if someone could design a clock that didn't look like a clock at all and signalled somehow on the hour (or the 50 minutes) I am sure every therapist in the country would buy one. Since most therapists use candles at some point in their work, how about a scented 'clock' candle? Perhaps a gadget that emitted a waft of sage oil on the hour would also be appropriate. I also await the appearance of the Bottomless Kleenex Box, disguised, perhaps, as a cushion.

We all have to stretch our brains at times to come up with ideas for specific clients - why not apply this ability to ourselves? (and if it's that brilliant, market it - see Section II).

How Much More Training Would You Like to Do?

When you increase the number of clients you see, you also increase the likelihood of your feeling de-skilled or inadequate. Therefore it is important to allow time for further training, professional workshops, and support groups throughout your career, if only to reassure you that what you do intuitively is correct.

Many holistic therapists (naturally enough) are trained in more than one discipline. Perhaps you are qualified in massage, addiction recovery counselling, rebirthing, astrology, sound therapy and in addition are a clairvoyant and a healer. You are equipped, you feel, for every possibility. Then you get four clients who are HIV positive, three who disclose childhood sexual abuse, a 'depressed' client who turns out to have M.E., and a GP refers to you a 'paranoid' client with recurrent candida who explains (perhaps after three sessions) that she is bulimic. Another informs you that you met in a past life and should now continue your love affair, and one day another gets in touch with his anger and threatens to wreck your consulting room.

All the training you have had cannot prepare you for the reality of daily work. You feel confident enough in your skills to cope with most eventualities, and as time wears on you realise that the more clients you see, the more you can hourly expect the unexpected. Clients present with increasingly complex, and often chronic, problems. Growing numbers of people are dissatisfied with the NHS and turn to complementary therapies; there are groups for survivors of the NHS mental health system along with groups for tranquilliser addicts and many other pharmacuetically-imposed iatrogenic conditions.

People in recovery from substance addictions often seek one-to-one therapy in addition to their work with self-help groups, and are willing to try several forms of natural therapy.

People with cancer, or AIDS-related conditions, or those living with HIV infection, have for many years been drawn to natural therapies, often with the support of their physicians. Whether your type of therapy is considered treatment or not, you will always have clients who have serious health conditions or serious emotional problems (and of course those with both, since one leads to the other).

Depending on your life/career plan, and on what sort of clients seem to be drawn to you (and who you are most drawn to) try and identify what your training needs will be in future. If you do not do this, you will find yourself often referring on clients who reveal material you do not feel able to work with. You will also, of course, during your career discover new interests and develop new talents. If you are a homoeopath, you may want to study psychotherapy, or do a course on past-life regression. Natural birth specialists may want to study acupuncture. As you develop your own body awareness you may want to take a dance course. The permutations are endless, which is what makes this such an interesting field to work in.

What do people ask you to do?

Probably nothing, except what is staring you in the face - the work you do now. A photograph or a mirror shows what you look like to others, so try and see yourself from your observers' points of view: no-one ever sees us the way we see ourselves. What do other people see in you? What do they ask you to do? Perhaps they see things that you didn't think important or relevant, or perhaps you have been so busy searching for the purpose of your life that you haven't noticed you are living it out now.

A very important thing to remember is that if people ask you to do things you haven't done before, it is probably because no-one they know is doing that, and they think you are the ideal person to do it. Furthermore there is probably a need for it.

You don't have to be perfect - you just need to be prepared to 'give it a go' as the Australians say. So next time someone asks you to do something you haven't done before, say 'yes'. If you are wanting to get more clients, and holding on to that, think for a moment about whether you want to expand your existing base or whether you want to go for something a little different.

In the same way that clients have confidence in you, and therefore (unknowingly) test and challenge you all the time, people who know you will assume that you are able to do all sorts of things, and they are probably right. Trust and value them, and listen to what they say. None of us know how much we know until life requires us to find out, such as someone asking us to do something we haven't done before.

Marketing and Promotion

What is marketing?

Marketing is the means whereby a business matches its services or products with the customers' needs. Practitioners sell a service. This means matching up your service to the needs of the people with whom you want to work. Marketing involves several processes, including:

- deciding what type of people your potential clients are
- how many of them there are
- what they need
- how much they can pay
- where they are
- how to reach them
- how to persuade them to buy what you are selling
- whether they will come to you or you to them
- and most important, *knowing that you and you alone can meet their particular needs.*

Research

One aspect of research is 'identifying a gap in the market'. This means finding out which group of clients are not getting what they need from what is presently available. You may then be able to fulfill this need. Research enables you *to identify* them *precisely*, discover what *influences* them and to find out where they are and *how to reach them.* Research can also mean having a great idea, then finding out if anyone else is already doing it. Or asking ten friends and colleagues what they think of this idea, whether they would 'buy' what you have on offer, under what circumstances and at what price. This could be something as straightforward as a mail-shot listing your proposed workshops, and asking recipients to tick off the ones they are interested in.

For the purposes of getting more clients, research also means finding out as much as you can about the world in which your prospective clients live/work, including trends and current affairs, being able to identify your ideal client, knowing what motivates them, targetting them accurately (that is, writing all your promotional material for them personally), knowing what or who influences them, knowing where they are, and how much money they have to spend on you.

Research could also mean asking each new client where they heard of you, and ask colleagues where their clients come from.

Professional marketers spend a great deal of time and money on *market research* to find out what products are needed. Once the product is perfected they then do 'test marketing' in selected areas - practicing the advertising and promotion and checking the response, usually by the number of sales which result. This is the normal course of events and absolutely essential for people (and businesses) who rely on selling a large number of consumer goods. What is being tested is the marketing style rather than the product: they already know people want the product because they have done all those months of research.

You are working with a specialist market in mind and doing what is known Out There as 'niche marketing'. As a member of this market yourself, you are in a much better position to relate to your potential clients than, say, is a director of Sainsbury's who is a squillionaire selling washing powder to working class families.

What you need to do in your market research is find out all you need to know about the people you want to reach so that you can 'target' them as individuals. Once you have a picture of your ideal client, you will know who you are talking to when you write your leaflet. You will also know how your ideal client would be likely to hear about you.

Unless you are trying to sell 100,000 copies of a book, we are not talking mass-marketing. We are talking about selective marketing in a specific, special field. Markeing in the 'holistic' field is 'personal' marketing, because you are marketing yourself as well as your work, because your work is an extention of you. You are selling yourself to people whom you know (not personally, but you know who they are and what they need). You are only looking for 12, 20, 50 clients at the most (unless you are planning a large centre, or you are an evangelist, or you want to do seminars).

You want to know the quickest way you can reach enough people for 20 (or whatever number you want) to become your clients.

How To Get More Clients

You are here, they are there - how do you make the connection? You will know you have succeeded when your clients recognise that it is you (your therapy, workshop, etc) that can meet their present need better than anyone else (and 'better' is a highly subjective word. It could mean 'cheaper' or 'nearer' or 'at the right time'. 'Better' in this sense means better for the client, rather than better than any other practitioner).

Marketing, especially advertising and promotion, costs money. Every pound you spend has to be got back to you quickly. Remember, though, that every pound you spend is an investment in yourself and in your business.

You will need to know something about the competition - your 'rivals'. The greater the competition, the more you need to build upon your uniqueness.

Golden Rules

Rule 1. *Locate your practice where potential clients are in abundance.* 'Location, location, location'. This are the words given to anyone thinking of opening a shop. *Where* you locate your shop is of crucial importance. To a large extent the same can be said of where you locate your practice. It is especially important for practitioners who see clients regularly on a one-to-one basis. Individual clients do not want to travel too far and expect to find a practitioner in the locale. Workshops are somewhat different as they are often held for just one weekend and clients are willing to travel. Therefore, if you want one-to-one clients, you need to locate your practice where your clients live or work. Firstly you need to determine what a typical client is like and then research where these potential clients live and work. A profile for a typical client who goes to therapy is: has a large disposable income, tends to be female (approximately 60% are women), middle class, white, often single, Guardian reader, lives in private rented or own home, between the ages of 25-55. This is of course a gross generalisation. To discover who your potential clients are, you can base it on what type of clients you already get and from that decide what is similar about them. Or you can draw up a profile of your potential client. (See a later exercise). Once you have got a good idea of who your potential clients are the next step is to find out where they live or work. It's probably best to go to that area and look around. Go on a Saturday to a shopping area in that locale and from just looking at the people milling around you should get a good impression of the type of people who live there. You should also see if there are any locations where the type of clients you are seeking may visit, e.g. wholemeal cafes, wholefood shops, New Age shops, independent cinemas.

There are marketing companies who deal in providing research data for you. If you provide them with the profile of a typical client then they will do a statistical seach of a geographic area and tell you the density of typical clients in that area and where the pockets of high density of clients lie. They charge a fee of approximately £300 to cover an area of up to 400 square miles. To find out about these agencies enquire at a large library. Libraries also carry statistic on census breakdowns which may be useful to you.

Rule 2. *Locate your practice where there are few similar practitioners.* Obviously if there is less competition the easier your life will be. The more competition there is the more unique your service needs to be. For instance if you are the only homoeopath in Birmingham then you only need to promote yourself as a homoeopath. If however there are 100 homoeopaths in Birmingham then you need to offer something that is different from the competition. Find out what the competition is like in your intended locale. Visit places where your competitors are likely to advertise and look in publications and noticeboards where you would expect to see them advertising their services. This will give you a good idea of the competition you can expect to be facing. If the locale seems crowded with practitioners that offer the same service as you then look elsewhere to set up a practice.

Rule 3. *Err on the side of over publicising yourself.* You can expect about a 1% response rate to any leaflets you produce offering your services. Many practitioners don't realise this and are disappointed at what they think is a poor response rate. It costs money and/or time to get known. Allocate 25% of your income to marketing and promotion. This expense should be costed into the fees you charge your clients.

Rule 4. *Target your clients.* Think small. Think of ten people you could phone who may be able to supply you with clients. It may be that you would suggest the names of fellow practitioners, a local GP, the owner of a local New Age bookshop. Phoning these people would be much more cost-effective than putting a full page advert in a specialist magazine. The advert would cost you approximately £500, the phone calls about £3, and you are more likely to get a better response from phoning.

Rule 5. *Find out what clients need and supply it.* If a potential client phones you up and asks about the type of therapy you do, then turn the conversation around to find out what they need. Ask 'why do you want massage', for example. If he/she were to say 'it's for may neck, I work with computers and my neck becomes very stiff', you are then in a position to say why your massage is good for that particular problem. Ask your prospective clients lots of questions to find out what they need. Getting a dialogue going is more likely to provoke a potential client's interest.

Rule 6. *Be unique.* The greater the competition in your locale, the more you need to build upon your uniqueness. For example if there are an abundance of massage practitioners and you practice massage, then build upon your uniqueness in offering 'intuitive massage'.

Rule 7. *Monitor where your clients come from.* When you get an enquiry from a prospective client ask them how they heard about you and keep a record. You will then be able to review your records and determine your best sources for clients (and your worst). This enables you to spend your promotional budget wisely by only backing what works.

Rule 8. *Don't sit back and expect clients to find you.* A myth, amongst psychotherapists in particular, is that clients will come to you when you are ready for it to happen. It's crap. Don't wait to be discovered. Get out there and make yourself known.

Rule 9. *Make yourself available.* A fear amongst practitioners is that they must appear successful to attract clients. They then resort to all manner of devices to pretend a full clientele when it is not so. This can has the opposite effect and put prospective clients off. Further, you should not put obstructions in the way of letting clients contact you. When you advertise include a phone number. Try to have a human answer the phone for you rather than an answerphone. If you do have to use an answerphone then respond to the message as soon as you can. Treat every incoming call as a potential sale.

Rule 10. *Build up a referal network and then service that network.* Monitoring where your clients come from will enable you to hone down your referral system. Once you have built up a steady referral system then you must service the referal system. If you are getting clients from practitioners you trained with then mail them regularly, keeping them up-to-date with what you are doing. Phone them for a chat and make sure to keep in touch. If you are getting your clients from a directory, make sure you know when the next edition is coming out to be sure not to be left out.

Rule 11. *Don't produce scrappy leaflets.* Give a lot of time to writing the copy so that it sounds good and make the leaflet look at least half-way respectable.

Rule 12. *Old clients are a source of new business.* It's an old adage that 80% of one's business comes from 20% of one's clients. So don't forget to keep those clients who regularly support you happy. Provide them with regular updates. Mail them regulary with news of what you are doing. Send them Valentine cards and kiss their feet if you have to, but do not forget about them. They are essential to your business.

Rule 13. *Don't lose heart.* In a recent survey in America, 50% of clients who came for a first interview for psychotherapy did not come back for a second session. Many people make a first appointment never to heard from again. Take heart from this. It's not you, it's the way things are.

Picturing your ideal client

To find your prospective clients you first must have some idea of who you are looking for. Describe your ideal client. This is the one who is going to be your next new client, or the first one to register for your workshop or group. She's a real person. Draw a picture of her, give her props. What does she usually do at the weekends? Does she live alone, or in a big house with other people of the same age, or is she in a steady partnership? How old is she? Does she have children? What are her home circumstances? How much spare cash does she have? Has she had therapy/been in a group/done workshops before? What does she read? Which newspaper or magazine; what type of books? Where does she usually buy them? How healthy is she?

What is her basic personality type? What hasn't she got that she can't do without? How does she perceive her future? How readily does she ask for help? Does she have supportive friends? What colours does she like in her home? What clothes does she wear? Does she follow fashions? Does she work? If so, at what? Is she a feminist? Is she heterosexual? What does she want to know? How far along her growth path is she? Is she depressed? Does she have a drinking problem? What does she think of allopathic medicine? What does she think of complementary medicine? Does she know what a chakra is?

Can she sing or draw or write or dance? Is she quiet or noisy, extrovert or introvert? Is she academic? Why would she want to experience your therapy/group/workshop? Would she rather come alone, or with a friend? Is she a student or a pensioner? What is her sex life like? What does she watch on TV? Does she eat out? Does she travel much? What sort of holidays does she prefer? Is she a giver or a taker? Does she know what she wants? Can you give it to her? Will she pay for it? Does she have secrets, fantasies? How does she feel about her childhood? What sort of music does she like? Does she read a lot? Is she anything like you? Who are her heroines/heroes?

Is it really necessary for you to know so much about your new client? Not always. If you know that 65 per cent of the population have bad backs, then all you need to do is advertise in the Yellow Pages that you can fix bad backs.

If it isn't that easy, what you need is a metaphorical 'bad back', something that will influence someone to look for treatment - and an 'influence' can be another person. The 'bad back' is the central feature of your marketing campaign, more importantly, your client's special type of 'bad back'. Making it better is the *need* you are going to meet.

When you are picturing your ideal clients, picture what will influence them to send off for your further information leaflet and then what will influence them to pay the deposit and commit themselves to the workshop.They will need to be so keen to come that they will send the cheque off at once to be certain of getting a place.

I know someone who always writes personal letters - she has nice, legible handwriting, of course. This works a charm, as her targetted clients are all people who need personal attention and love. If someone writes you a letter with an an enquiry about your therapy, it is important to reply to all the points raised. There are, after all, people who do not feel confident on the telephone and if they have written, write back, don't phone, and do mark the envelope 'personal'.

Targetting your clients

Accurate targetting is important as it can save money spent on printing thousands of leaflets and even more money spent on advertising in the wrong publication. It also means you can estimate how many people will respond to whatever promotion you are doing. Targetting helps you to be consistent, from the creation of your workshop, therapy style, group or product, to the design and writing of your leaflet, to where you work and all the other essentials of successful practice.

If you are beginning to feel befuddled with choices and information, and trying to work out what applies to you, then this just how your clients feel as they become more aware of the enormous variety of therapies on offer to them.

Just as you select which parts of this guide are relevant to you, so your potential clients will shuffle through leaflets and advertisements looking for something that enables them to say 'That's for Me'. What makes them say this is the feeling that you understand them. 'Your leaflet struck a chord with me', they might say, or 'It leapt out at me from the shelf'. They may not know what they are looking for till they see it.

You can help them to see it by *targetting them specifically*. Remember, you are only aiming for 10, 20, or perhaps 50 people.

Where do you begin? There are several good starting points and you will probably have your own ideas as well. By now you should know what type of clients you want. You will need more than one 'target' because you want to be *certain* of attracting a minimum number of clients. If you do more than one type of work you will need more target groups, and the more you know about them the better because for each group you will need slightly different types of promotion. Think about the most cost-effective ways of reaching them.

As well as people who are likely to become your clients, there is a sub-group to consider as well. This consists of people who may or may not be in the holistic business, and are in a position to *influence* potential clients. This sub-group is extremely important and may a require different approach in terms of how you market yourself to them. It may include other practitioners who will refer clients to you, GPs and past clients who will recommend to their friends.

Large companies with hundreds of products allot huge annual budgets to working out who is in which consumer group, and they keep records of types of purchasers by all sorts of cunning systems: competitions in certain newspapers, special offers in others,and different levels of promotion in different areas. I will now, for a mere fraction of the cost, tell you some of these methods. Not all, of course as it is an exhausting subject. The 'New Age' media does not collect the sort of statistics required for readership analyses and other details which the advertiser of a mass-market product would expect. The best we can do is ask around and see what results colleagues achieved from different outlets.

Where are the clients in your locality?

Unless they are setting up huge or once-in-a-lifetime events, most practitioners expect their clients to live within reasonably easy reach of their practices. The nearer clients live, the more likely they are to be able to come regularly, rather than their appointment with you requiring a special trip. In addition, you need to know what else in your area is likely to attract their attention, and, most important in marketing terms, where to site your posters, leaflets and other promotion.

Draw a circle around you on a map of your area.

This is your 'A' target, geographically speaking. Your 'B' target will be a larger circle around it. Obviously in a city your circle will be much smaller than if you are in a rural district. What falls into that circle? Rows and rows of suburban houses? Several adult education centres? A shopping complex? Lots of bookshops? A golf course and a leisure centre? Farmland? What sort of business are in your chosen area? Light industry? Warehouses? An airport? The centre of commerce of your city? Small shops? Tea shops? Sixteen more natural health centres? A zoo? A theme park? Several theatres, cinemas and discos? If the locale does not look too fertile, you will need a bigger circle.

Who comes into your circle? Do all the people who work there also live there, or do they commute? Alternatively, does everyone who lives there work elsewhere? Who is left behind all day and what is there in the locality to do with their time? Where they go is where they are likely to see your leaflet.

What is there in your circle which is big enough to have a staff notice board, such as a college, hospital, a radio station or the Town Hall? And probably the most important question of all: where do the present users of your services come from?

If you are working in an area unfamiliar to you, local libraries have lists of everything in the district classified alphabetically. Anything funded by the local health authority or local Government has to be listed and categorised and the information distributed freely. In this way you will find what other facilities, including free ones, are available to your potential clients. If there are 2000 osteopaths already, you need to say in your leaflet why you are special. If there is a medical herbalist training school two streets away, you need to detail your experience and any special applications of your herbal medicines, or perhaps set up a dispensary, plus mentioning other therapies that you do - and finding out if the training centre needs you! If there are 5,000 masseurs or crystal healers, all working from home, so start a centre, or a networking magazine or New Age bookshop, and sell them lots of copies of this book.

For any therapist, it is quite a shock to discover what else is going on in the area. There are parts of London, for instance, where if you are likely to find one Natural Health Centre you are likely to find a dozen. Everyone else seems to have got there first. Don't worry, keep remembering that you are unique - you must be doing something they are not doing. It may be something simple like a shorter waiting time for treatment, later hours, or Saturday morning clinics.

Always remember that even in West Hampstead therapists are making a living.

What influences people?

What influences people in choosing a particular therapy or in choosing one particular practitioner? You have to know what the 'influence' is, because people are unsure about giving up their time and money for something that they cannot sit and look at, show to friends, wear, or give away as a present. People need to be driven by quite a strong inner need in order to spend money on themselves. (For details of how to establish influences in different target groups, see below).

We live in such a materialistic society, that you have to sell whatever you do as a 'thing' that people can take away with them. The 'thing' can be better health, a training, or an answer to a question that's been puzzling them, or ideas on how to get a better job, have a better relationship, or a tool to fix their pain. Some'thing' that will help them change their lives for the better, or provide them with a meaning for their existence and a purpose in their lives.

How to assess influences

Advertising agencies classify people by their social class, in order to work out what potential customer groups will be influenced by. Perhaps a more appropriate way of doing this for the purposes of therapies is to consider which of the three following categories your potential clients fall into. My system of 'people types' which I offer below, have little to do with social class, wealth or formal education.

Group A: People who make their own choices, and may have already made a choice about what type of therapy, group, workshop or course they want. They will look for it, ask around. Depending on their circle of contacts they might ask friends, another therapist, someone they meet at a fair, a helpline, a magazine, a community centre, health food shop and many other likely sources of information, especially a natural health centre if there is one in their area. Networks are another good starting point. In other words, *these potential clients know where to look.* Group A people have probably experienced some sort of therapy, read books and articles about complementary medicine, given thought to improving their health, lifestyle and environment, worked out how much they can spend on themselves, have been to one or more holistic fairs, receive mail-shots from one or more sources, browse in alternative bookshops, are creative, have decided there is more to life than doing what everyone else does, are prepared to be individuals at the risk of feeling lonely. They may or may not accept New Age beliefs. They may be therapists or student therapists.

Group B: People who generally go for what other people recommend - personal contacts, members of the media, or other practitioners. They also look in professional association directories, found in libraries or doctors' surgeries. They may have done some of the Group A activities, though have less of a commitment to the holistic lifestyle. They probably eat and drink what they want, read the health and 'pop' psychology articles in newspapers and magazines and have at some time attended classes such as yoga for health, aerobics, Tai Chi or dance. They work and probably socialise with their colleagues, they know when they are not well and what remedies work for them. They are interested in new things, in finding out about themselves, and in creating better relationships. They go to holistic fairs, health shows, or psychics and mystics fairs. They are socialists at heart and believe in self-empowerment. They enjoy group activities.

Group C. These are people who don't know that they want therapy (or a group, workshop, etc). They come from widely divergent social groups. Either they are in life to make money, and don't believe in any sort of therapy (until they get ill or their marriages break up) or they are underpriveleged, with low self-esteem, with a belief that illness comes from outside them and that the cure must come from someone who knows about these things. They read the horoscope columns and pop psychology articles in newspapers and magazines, and possibly books recommended by these articles. They would rather have astrology, a psychic or Tarot reading, a massage or a one-off counselling session than any form of therapy that requires them to change their lifestyle. They would not go to personal growth workshops and feel slightly nervous of the New Age. They might go to interesting talks, hoping their problem is mentioned, but are usually too shy to ask about it if it isn't. They come from families where any kind of unusual behaviour is described as 'neurotic', and are very scared of 'mental illness'. If they feel depressed, they would deny it, saying they have a headache or that they are 'coming down with something'. Their boundaries are vague, they feel guilty sometimes, and probably eat too much.

Never underestimate people in this group - once they discover the possibilities life holds for them, they leap so quickly that you won't recognise them (and their families or colleagues are the first to say 'This isn't like you').

You will need to employ a different approach to reach people in each of these three groups.

What do people need?

While we all respond to the various infuneces in our lives, we are also strongly motivated to get our needs met. Marketing guru Andrew Ferguson of *The Breakthrough Centre* states that there are seven basic human needs to be fulfilled, and these apply to products and services, as well as therapies or workshops.

The Seven Needs are:

Instant solutions NOW is more important than perfection. Potential clients will want to know about 'performance' - *what it will do for them.*

Thrills that is, personal power, ego-boosting, reassurance, love, confidence-building and encouraging personal growth and *enhancing self-image.* 'I can do that!'

It works! Security, efficiency. Your potential clients will want to know that lots of other (authoritative) people have tried it and say *it works well.* It has to be presented in a safe, reliable, efficient and water-tight way, and have been tried and tested (perhaps by 'years of research'), and found to be do exactly what it says it will do.

Fun also known as joy, i.e. *the quality of the social/human aspects of your service.* These potential clients also like comfort, personal service and warmth, rather than cold, detached efficiency and analysis.

Mental stimulation anything of riveting interest, new, specificially for them, plenty of choice and lots of discussion about possible options. 'Products' need to be *complex and intriguing,* requiring their own skill and knowledge to be applied to the process.

Beauty that is, anything aesthetically appealing, elegant, stylish and of good design - which includes clever solutions

- and anything else which will result in appreciation by the beholder.

Inspiration which means being in touch with one's higher self, insight, creativity, change, and transformation. I would include here a sudden realisation of one's true Self. Superficiality and basics are out of the question here. Purity, love and peace, harmony and the progression of the human race (nothing less) is the required vision. I would add that people who want fun and mental stimulation are also candidates for love and harmony as well.

This is a good basic guide when you are trying to work out what your service, product or workshop needs to offer. As we know, the more people move along their growth paths, the more parts of themselves they discover, and so the *more* needs they have. There comes a point when you need to be able to meet all seven.

Personal needs

In terms of personal development human beings also have essential needs which workshop leaders, in particular, try to address. These needs are:

1. To feel secure
2. To ask for and find information (to communicate)
3. To feel valued, acknowledged and accepted and to have a sense of accomplishment
4. To be free to make choices, have fun, and to give and receive care and love
5. To be self-directing and self-expressing
6. To have a sense of purpose and fulfillment
7. To find meaning in life.

Setting Your Fees

There are three ways of determining the fees you charge for your services: (1) charge what the market will bear. Applied to your clients this means charging what you think clients are willing to pay. This depends on how unique, or how much in demand what you do is (2) work out your salary and expenses, and set your fees to cover this (3) charge a fee that is in line with what your competitors are charging. Check out how much a practitioners who offer a similar service to yourself are charging and set your fees on a par with them.

Cost is one of the 'influences' - not too cheap to appear tatty, not to expensive to appear exploitative. On the other hand if we truly want something, we don't care how much it costs, which is why you can charge more for something that is unique or necessary.

Here we go back to your ideal client. How much money would she be prepared to spend on herself? How much does she value herself and value what you do? You must find people who want your services more than a holiday, new VCR, training course, new sofa or whatever is currently tempting them.

If people want you, and you alone, cost is not the issue. If you can move people, that is, tug at the heart strings, or perhaps their solar plexi, they will find the money somehow (anyone who is still paying off the bank loan or second mortgage they took out in order to pay for their training would agree with me). Andrew Ferguson at the Breakthrough centre states *if your clients do not express a sharp intake of breath when you mention your fee* then you are probably not charging enough. If what you offer is unique then people will pay (where else can they go to find what you offer?).

If you price yourself too cheaply you will get clients who are just 'trying you out' and always choose the cheapest available. If you price yourself too highly, you will still get clients, however you will need to direct your publicity at clients who have enough spare Disposable Pounds. Or offer a 'once in a lifetime' experience, and understand that you will never see the same clients again.

The important thing about budgeting is that whatever you charge has to cover your costs, and you have to make a profit. As well as paying yourself, you have to pay for everything else. If you are self-employed you have to pay for every stamp, every envelope, every phone call, every towel, every typewriter ribbon, every piece of print, everything. Part of your earnings goes in tax and National Insurance stamps. You may be paying consulting room rent as well as a mortgage or rent for your home. If you are beginning your career, remember that you will only be keeping just over half of your income - much less if you are repaying a bank loan for your study fees.

Unless you are truly altruistic and can afford to be so, you are not here to subsidise your clients. You may want to do low-cost or voluntary work part of the time, and hopefully in a supportive environment. In which case you are not doing it for nothing, you are doing it for love. The rest of the week you need to be earning good money.

There are some therapists, of course who charge exploitative rates, using their positions of need to make the client pay well over the going rate. I heard of one psychotherapist who charged an anorexic client (or rather, the client's parents) £86 an hour in 1991. I hope that the more open we are, and the more discriminating and knowledgable clients become, these sort of fees will only apply to multi-millionaires.

You have the Promotional Skills

Promotion requires you to present yourself for scrutiny. This is how you sell your services, either to potential clients, or to those who influence them. It is, therefore, something you can only do in a way which you enjoy, as you will otherwise appear unconvincing..

There is no point traipsing around exhibitions or fairs if you hate doing this, no more than it would be necessary to write long explanatory brochures if doing so is pure agony.

Quite separate from your professional competence, you already possess numerous natural promotion skills and marketing tools, though you may not yet have identified these personal assets in this way.

To identify your your best self-promotion skill, ask yourself some questions. What do people whom you know, and your existing clients, best *respond* to? Is it your sparkling eyes? Your 'Earth-motherliness'? Your strong, centred, physical appearance? Your aura of tranquillity? Your shyness? Your healing presence? Unpredictability? Your intelligence? Your humility? Your insight? Your poetic way with words?

Try defining your basic personality type and the way you work. Are you mostly practical, constructive and grounded; intuitive, creative and imaginative; logical, communicative, lively and quick-thinking? Sensitive, receptive, empathic and slightly shy?

What do people seem to want *you* for? What do friends say they like about you? Be warned; what they say can come as a bit of a surprise and this will tell you either that you don't know yourself very well, or (more likely) that you have successfully separated yourself from your work. Ten different people will say ten different things about you. Fine, so you have ten different arresting qualities. All of them can be used for promotion.

What is the effects you usually have on people and how do they feel about you? Stimulated, rested, drained, overpowered, stronger, more caring or cared about? Do they feel safe with you? Excited in a pleasant way? Jealous of you? Annoyed at your articulacy and insight? Does the sight of you result in people getting in touch with their prejudices? If you are a member of a minority group you will know that everyone is prejudiced about someone. You may even have decided that the prejudices your clients express is so sickening that you only want to work in your own community. However, your cultural background can give you considerable advantages.

As so many of the 'new' therapies were learned from older and wiser peoples, many practitioners find that their ancestry enables them to bring an authentic presence to their work, for instance if they are giving workshops on North American Indian healing rituals, or teaching Chinese or Ayurvedic Medicine.

How can personality traits and qualities be used as self-promotion skills?

If you are a very talky and commanding person, you could give talks about your type of therapy. If you write well, and hate talking, you can produce wonderful leaflets and write articles about yourself. There are hundreds of network bulletins, free local newspapers and other publications which welcome contributions from people who don't ask for any money. This can lead to better things: there is an astrologer who offered free horoscope columns to the early freesheets who had a pleasant surprise when the publishers started to pay £8 a column. A pittance, you may think. However, this column was syndicated in 120 of that publishers' local freesheets, so he received (weekly!) £960 for a column that took him an hour a week to write, and became nationally known, which, along with all the other self-promotion he was doing, led to him becoming extremely famous. Good things come in small packages.

If it is your sparkly eyes, which make you irresistible, always use a photograph of yourself on your leaflets, even on your cards. It may cost more, but it's well worth it. If you are very centred and earthed, you may feel more at ease with giving hands-on demonstrations at fairs or at centre open days. You could also consider teaching, if you enjoy showing other people how to do things and enjoy it when they learn.

If you are at the beginning of your career, you will know that hard work promoting yourself will pay dividends in the future. As well as offering yourself to the local adult education centre, you could write to various groups, nurses' homes or charities in the area suggesting talks demonstrations or mini-courses. Public interest in natural therapies is high and will continue to increase, so a short talk on, say, what to put in a natural health medicine cupboard would be of great interest, and you may be able to sell homeopathic first-aid kits, bottles of Rescue Remedy or bags of herbal teas. You could organise this in co-operation with a local health food shop so that you are not left with boxes of unsold remedies.

If it is your voice which impresses people, and you don't feel very confident about talking to large gatherings, you can try getting yourself interviewed on radio, including hospital radio. And there is always the telephone: if you like chatting away to friends, and are feeling nervous about giving your first workshop, you can give yourself and your clients confidence by ringing them up with the excuse of confirming the booking. In this way, you and they get to know each other a little.

And, of course, you may find an original or unusual promotion route than no-one else ever uses.

Promotion Ideas

Talks and demonstrations

Giving talks is a good way of finding clients. It's a chance for potential clients to meet you whilst remaining anonymous. So it is safe for them and they are likely to be influenced by seeing you in person.

There are one or two ground rules, the main one being: Don't panic! The people who come along area already interested in what you are going to say. You can use lots of 'props' to entertain people, and you don't have to do all the work. If you are an osteopath you can use a skeleton and big charts showing human anatomy, or if you are an iridologist, show gigantic colour blow-ups of the eye. Reflexology charts are easy to come by, and you can ask everyone to take their shoes and socks off and wiggle their toes. Palmists can get the audience involved in waving their hands around and flexing their fingers. You could pass around aromatherapy oils and ask people to smell them and try and describe how they feel.

You don't have to give 'lectures'. Depending on the equipment available at the chosen centre. You could give a slide show, or show a video about your therapy, and simply answer questions. If there is a flip chart available and you have plenty of brightly coloured markers, you could start with asking the audience what they know about your therapy and writing what they say on the flip chart. This is a wonderfully calming device for people who need to spend the first 15 minutes of giving a talk with their back to the audience! I like giving talks, however. When I first started, I would worry all week about what I was going to say and arrive with ten pages of notes. I soon found that I only used half of the first page; the rest of the time was taken up with questions and discussions. I also discovered that everyone in the room was much more self-conscious than I was. Start with some sort of ice-breaker, such as asking everyone to close their eyes and imagine themselves in their favourite, safe place. This relaxes you and the audience, and suggest the audience breaks into small groups to discuss a point, and then feed back. This is very effective.

Talks work best when you can demonstrate, on willing volunteers, what your therapy does. Hypnotherapy is an obvious example of this. Massage is another, and you can now buy 'on-site' massage equipment which enables the recipient to be seated, and not have to take their clothes off. Perhaps the line should be drawn at rebirthing, however! For a talk on healing, or auras, nothing is more effective than giving the audience a chance to sense each others' auras, and a group meditation (even if you call it a visualisation) is a powerful experience. If you are not sure you will have volunteers, take a friend along as a 'model'.

Expect questions at talks. Arrive well-prepared, and practice (with friends) thinking on your feet.

Previous contacts

All the tips I have given so far have concentrated on promoting yourself within your *new* field. However, you had a life before; studies, work, personal contacts, a community. Don't forget to tell them all what you are now doing and where you are working.

The best referral network you can ever have is personal contacts.

People who know you were good at what you did before will accept (whether or not they believe in what you are doing) that you are good at your new job as well, and a nice person too. They may ask you to do things that are outside your original type of work; however, it is often good to say 'yes'.

I learned this trick from my freelance journalism days, when editors would ring and ask me if I knew anything about 'this new thing digital sound', or did I know what a video camera was and could I write a book about how to make video movies, or what the new Copyright Act or the new Children Act meant, or what withholding tax was, or the real meaning of practitioner accreditation. I would always cheerfully say 'Yes' (thinking of the cheque) and then set about becoming an Instant Expert, since I had not the foggiest idea what any of it meant. Necessity, as one knows, is the mother of invention. You never know where it might lead, as the universe works in strange ways send things in odd packages.

Remember that work, and completely unexpected work opportunities, can come to you from any source, and that your personal and previous work contacts feed you clients (or other work offers) from time to time, and will probably remain resources for you of one sort or another all your working life.

A note of confusion

Now that 'accreditation' has becomes a buzzword for 'good therapist' (though that isn't necessarily what it means), charities, helplines, local authority training officers, health worker support groups, GPs and the like tend to look for the magic asterisk in the resource directories published by the professional associations. If you are not yet accredited, or your association does not have such a scheme, then it may be a waste of your time to go for these professional contacts. Ask your regional or local health authority what their policy is before sending dozens of letters or making fruitless and demoralising telephone calls.

Specific promotion

Below is a quick guide to various ways of spreading the word. There are as always different rules for different types of activities, so these are listed separately. Many practitioners take part in more than one activity. They see individual clients, set up centres, teach, train, run groups, hold workshops, and produce films, write books, and make and sell tapes or videos as well.

Individual clients:

- give talks about your type of therapy
- do locum work
- local newspaper articles about you
- being in the right place (locale and setting)
- holding workshops and groups
- circulating cards and leaflets
- giving full credentials and any speciality, to other professionals - GPs, health centres, nurses' homes, charities and self-help trusts, well-woman clinics, natural health clinics, sports centres, health 'clubs', active birth centres, adult education centres

- being listed in the main holistic directories, professional association directories, local resource lists, Yellow Pages and Thompson's Directory, Talking Pages, Holistic London, Whole Person Catalogue, etc.
- distributing your leaflet at holistic health fairs
- contacting religious groups
- creating a course
- reminding the centre where you trained where you are working
- 'What's On' listings in the local newspaper and any other relevant papers/magazines, including specialist health and fitness magazines, listings magazines, women's pages, and network magazines
- telling-every single person you know what you are doing and where you are working
- being in a network which shares advertising and answerphone costs
- writing brochures about your type of therapy and distributing them to local centres, public libraries, adult education centres, alternative bookshops and other 'congregation points'
- find out if there is a network local to you which produces a bulletin. This may be somewhere you can advertise, though it is more likely that it is put together by a group of practitioners or a local centre to spread the word, that is, network, throughout an area.
- Get interviewed on the radio.
- Sell a product and get known through it.
- Do other related part-time work e.g. teach your therapy and get clients from students
- Make contact with local holistic health centres and let them know you exist and you are available to see clients.

- Mailshot GPs. The library have a list of local GPs or use the Yellow Pages to find addresses.
- Run specialist courses for professionals e.g. doctors, nurses etc. They will then refer clients to you.
- Run a training. Many clients are interested in training. The trainees become good referral sources for you.
- Put a notice up on noticeboards. Make sure it's not tatty.
- Work out where potential clients congregate and advertise or promote yourself there.
- Build up a network of referral sources. For example do deals with other practitioners. Refer if distance makes travel difficult.
- Take over a clientele from another practitioner. Not a hostile takeover you understand, but if you stay in touch with practitioners whose practice is similar to yours then you might end up with the clientele if the therapist wants a sabbatical, changes career, goes on holiday or spontaneously combusts.
- Make it known that you are available to see clients. Tell everyone.
- Write a book related to the therapy you practice. You will then become an expert and a side benefit is that you can sell the book to your clients.
- Produce a leaflet and get it distributed.
- Advertise. Ways too numerous to mention.
- Let relevant retail outlets know that you are a practitioner. Give them free sesssions and they may refer customers to you. e.g. back furniture shop if you are an osteopath.
- Contact people you trained with and ask them if they will refer clients to you.
- Take over the administration of the referral service you trained with and syphon off a few clients for yourself.

- Set up a magazine or newsletter in your speciality and promote yourself through this.
- Keep a mailing list of all past and present clients, anyone who enquires, referral sources etc and mail them regularly.
- Swap mailing lists with other practitioners or do co-operative mailings ('I'll mail your leaflet if you'll mail mine').
- As hospitals now buy in services, make yourself known to your local hospital.
- Ask your friends to refer you clients.
- Write articles for magazines and local papers. Freebies will often print an 'advertorial'.
- Offer companies a service e.g. massage for computer operators.
- Tell your present clients you have available spaces and ask them to refer you clients.

Group workshop members:

As above, and note the following. Notices about your group should be sent, well in advance, to as many centres as you feel are appropriate. In addition, you need to list groups in network bulletins, and, for long-term therapy groups, even more in advance in the relevant quarterly publications, plus your local listing magazines (if they have a personal growth section). Leaflets can be sent (or notices put up in) to natural health centres, public libraries, health food shops, training centres, adult education and community centres, your own training centre, every other therapist you know and several who you don't know, local helplines, mental health charities, and alternative bookshops.

Minorities:

If you are serving a particular minority market, you will want to circulate all the relevant organisations/centres/publications/resource listings which serve that minority group, as well as some of the general outlets already mentioned. As a member of a minority group yourself, you will know where/what these are. In addition, don't forget your local council, trade union and Health Service Equal Opportunities officers. There are dozens of community newspapers which run free listings. In the past five years, in which I have received thousands of leaflets through the post, I cannot remember seeing a workshop or group advertised specifically for black women (for example) or any other ethnic minority group - or any minority group, for that matter. If I want to find out about these, or my clients do, they need to contact community centres and publications or networks serving the needs of their particular special group. It seems that positive discrimination is only excercised by publicly-funded organisations, such as helplines, women's centres, drug and alcohol counselling services, charities, or NHS clinics.

Workshops:
As above under 'individual clients' and note the following. Mailshots, notices in (mainly) natural health centres and therapy training centres; advertisements (months in advance) in therapy magazines; centres producing lists of forthcoming workshops to give to individual clients and to mail out; network bulletins; advertisements in local papers; listings in magazines and everything else mentioned above. Workshops are a special case and have a detailed section of their own.

Psychotherapy
Technically included in the guidelines above for individual clients, they are also a special case. The reason is that natural health practitioners have a greater turnover of clients than psychotherapists (and counsellors). In this way, psychotherapists, theoretically, have less of a need for the continual advertising and promotion than natural health practitioners. However, if you are building up a client list, the suggestions in the first paragraph will apply to you. Psychotherapists also run groups, hold workshops, give talks, write articles and books, run seminars, attend accreditation meetings, go to support groups, attend conferences, take courses, go for massage and shiatsu, and probably teach and do supervision as well (in their spare time). Now you know why they charge such high fees. The point is that *they get known by other psychotherapists*, the most effective form of networking. In addition, they have (or have had)

their own therapist and their supervisor, both of whom are good sources of clients - the ones they cannot take on themselves. Though, in many trainings, trainers and teachers are not allowed to have trainees as clients. Knowing other psychotherapists is important because sometimes colleagues go abroad, or take a sabbatical, or get ill, and if their clients want to continue in therapy, they need to be referred on to someone personally recommended. The same thing happens, or course, to other practitioners who recommend a colleague to take over their practices.

Whatever your work, stay in touch with your training centre. Some of these have assessment therapists who sees all potential clients, and then passes them onto to a therapist he/she feels is right for the client.

Other professionals

Practitioners who work from home and rely on a steady flow of one-off clients tend to advertise in local newspapers and in magazines specific to their healing arts. Many work one day a week in a small natural health centre, or perhaps in rooms above an alternative bookshop. Some join networks and take stands at holistic fairs, often travelling all over the country together. Some put up cards in local shop windows, and others are in national organisations, such as the National Federation of Spiritual Healers, or the British Astrological Society.

Where do potential clients look for you?

Ten years or so ago, it was difficult for clients to know where to start looking for therapists. Some would ask their doctor, others would search around for a health food shop or what were then known as alternative bookshops.

Now it is considerably easier, as there is so much publicity, and people are much more aware of the choices available. All you need to do is to make sure that your card or leaflet is in the right place.

Potential clients seem to have a sense of where to look. If they don't know their way round the holistic world, they start with listings magazines that have a personal growth or courses section (reputable ones ask advertisers for copies of their certificates). There is even a magazine now called *Courses*. Women might look in *Spare Rib* or *Everywoman,* or one of the women's directories, or go to a women's centre. Most people know that alternative bookshops stock copies of the various personal growth and health magazines. They look in telephone directories and Yellow Pages (or local equivalent), Thompsons', the local paper, library notice boards and health food shop notice-boards. They also still ask their doctors, and if a centre advertises an open day, they go to that. Many go to holistic fairs. All of these are therefore potential promotional outlets.

If you are a therapist working in a minority community, you will have discovered that the professional bodies do not have a category for you. If you are a gay or lesbian therapist, you will be offered membership of, perhaps, the Sexual, Family and Marital section, despite perhaps specialising in eating disorders. Some of the gay and lesbian centres and helplines have lists of therapists, and I have been unable to find out if there is one central list despite several months of research. Is there a type of prejudice out there, or indeed, within the profession, which gives the impression that there are no black, disabled, gay or lesbian therapists, natural health practitioners, crystal healers, art therapists, or astrologers? We know this is nonsense, of course, and it is infuriating for a client who wants to see someone they can relate to, rather than someone who might pathologise their difference.

Leaflets and other promotional ephemera

The Ubiquitious Leaflet has become the favoured, and usually the most effective, form of promoting therapies, workshops, courses, centres, fairs, new initiatives and products. They have become more and more elaborate, more colourful and more glossy, though leaflets for individual therapy and many workshops seem to remain somewhat drab - typed and photocopied, perhaps. The leaflet has generated its own sub-industry and there is now a whole army of support services, one of which is *Direct Mail.*

Direct mail can mean sending a magazine to subscribers, accompanied by a leaflet. While there have always been quarterly magazines, or the bulletins of the various holistic associations and networks, there are now several mailing firms which exist solely to send out leaflets.

Direct mail requires careful thought. As the holistic world grows and becomes more and more varied, you can't be certain who is getting all the magazines, unless they are only going to members of a professional association, say. With the mailing firms however, you have some choice about who leaflets are going to. A mistake commonly made by new practitioners is to contact somebody famous who does regular mail-outs and ask to be included in their next one. This person may send out 15,000 leaflets every quarter, and this long list will include everyone who has ever come to any of their workshops. You don't need this many, and it certainly isn't cost-effective. 6,000 is ample for most one-off workshops or short courses which have a target of about 20 clients. A guru visiting the UK sent 100,000 leaflets, shared with three other workshops leaders, in the same mail shot as a famous exhibition. He had three bookings. What he didn't know (or didn't ask?) was that all the workshops in that mail shot were on the same weekend.

Work out the sums involved

Generally expect a response rate of 1% if you are distributing your leaflets in magazines or other peoples mailouts. A response rate of 2% is good, 4% unusually good. If you own your own list and you intend to do follow-up phone calls to those people you have sent leaflets to you can get the response rate up to 10%. If you are sending out to people who have asked to be informed about your services and who expressed a strong interest and you do a follow-up phone call you can get the response rate up to 30%. Some companies operate and make a profit on a response rate of 0.3%.

You should calculate whether it's worth doing a mail shot. Work out the response rate you need to break even. For example if you mail out to 1000 people about a weekend workshop you intend to run, the sums add up as follows:
Cost of stamps = £180
Cost of envelopes = £50
Cost of labour to stuff envelopes and mail (at £5 per hour) = £40
Cost to typeset leaflet =£30
Cost of printing leaflet = £40
TOTAL = £340
If you expect a response rate of 1%, 10 clients will respond. Assuming all book (which is unlikely) then at £65 per workshop you will sell £650 of space. Subtract the mailing cost from this and you are left with (£650 - £340)= £310, from which you must also deduct other expenses, such as the cost of the room and the cost in labour in putting the leaflet together. Obviously you won't make a lot of money this way, so what can you do to improve this? Well you can

(1) reduce the cost of the mailing. You can do this by putting your leaflet in someone else's mailing (known as a co-operative mailing), this reduces the cost as the postage and envelopes are shared. Or you could take others leaflets in your mailout and charge them for this service.

(2) increase the response rate. To increase the response rate aim to get a better mailing list which reaches your target audience more effectively, or design a more attractive leaflet with better copy. Companies get up to all kinds of schemes to increase the response rate, such as offering free gifts, prize draw, discounts if respondents book early etc.

(3) increase the price of the workshop. Do be careful not to undercharge. You can work out if your undercharging by

working out your break even point. You should not drop below it.

(4) offer more workshops or items that they can buy in the same mailing. If you offer two worshops then this is likely to increase the response rate as respondents are likely to have more of a choice. It may be that they could not make that particular weekend due to prior engagements.

As you can see from the above figures, putting together a leaflet promoting only one workshop does not make economic sense, unless you get spin-offs from this (such as individual sessions booked, or selling those respondents further workshop space). It makes much more sense to offer a series of workshops, and individual sessions as well on the same leaflet.

It may be that if you only get one person respond to a mailing of 1,000 intended to reach potential individual clients you will make a profit. If that clients stays with you for two years, seeing you once a week at £25 per session then your income from this is approximately £2500. Thus from a response rate of only one tenth of one per cent you could do very well. To work out your break-even figure for direct mail in getting individual clients you must first work out how much you make on average from each potential client. To work this out go back over your records and count up the *average* amount you make from each person who first contacts you for an individual session. One potential client may have stayed for several years, but others get no further than a phone call, and if potential clients don't show for the first interview then this loss of income to you must be reflected in the average. The average amount may well come as a shock. Let us say for examples sake that the average is £100. Then if you get a response rate of 1% to 1,000 leaflets you stand to get sales of £1000. From this you must deduct the cost of the leaflets to give you a gross profit.

Why leaflets are so important

Your leaflet is the bridge between you and your clients. It is the first step in your building a relationship (however short) with them. What they hold in their hands, what they see and read, and what they feel about it, is usually all that they have with which to decide whether or not to become your clients. The leaflet may be the first they have heard of you, or it may be at the end of their chain of enquiry. It must therefore (a) attract people to it (b) make them read it and (c) *transform them from casual passer-by to client.*

Your leaflet should never be 'a shot in the dark'. The *look* of it - colour, design, typeface, illustrations, the *feel* of it - the type of paper used, and the *text* to be read, and the general *impression* (or image) it conveys all have to express who you are and the way in which you work.

The most important thing your leaflet must demonstrate is your complete faith in yourself and what you are offering. For workshop leaders in particular, brief details of how the method worked for you, and why, is extremely effective. You are living proof that the method or therapy works. If you don't believe much of what you are writing, nor will your readers. If you are uncertain, or cautious, or worried as you write, this will come across in your writing. Be positive, direct, personal, and disarming.

In addition, the leaflet must contain practical information - where to get hold of you, where you are working (and the advantages and special features of the venue), time limit for bookings and cancellations, payment requirements (deposit for workshops/courses, or fees scale for individual sessions), details of your therapy, and anything the client needs to bring along.

A good set of rules to use is commonly known as AIDA, which stands for Attention, Interest, Desire, Action. The leaflet must first gain the *attention* of the reader. This is usually done by putting the heading in large type and in bold. It should also be worded so as to grab the attention of the reader. Do not use the company name here. *The Institute of Rebirthing and Past Life Therapy* will not grab the readers' attention. Secondly you should aim to arouse *Interest* in the reader by telling her more about what you are offering. Thirdly arouse *Desire*; aim to hook the part of them that says 'I want this'. Finally stir them to *Action.* This is often done by saying places are limited or offering a discount if they book early. Humour and graphics also help.

The amount of information given depends on whether this is the first leaflet or whether it is the 'further details' sent off for by someone who has seen a poster, advertisement, listing or initial mail shot. And 'information' does not have to be in writing - you can say a great deal with an illustration, a photograph, a symbol, the design, typography and writing style, the amount of space you leave, the colour of the paper and the printing ink, and the type of paper you use. Some people are able to make these choices instinctively, others work it out by trial and error, others copy leaflets that they like, others follow the rules.

Though it most of us work on a very low budget, it seems a shame to skimp on a leaflet which is advertising your professional services after spending many years and much money and effort on training, equipment, and premises. To a certain extent a tatty leaflet can work for you, e.g. if your client group are normally alienated by anything that looks 'official'. However, since most of us need to earn money we must assume that people who have the money to spend are used to seeing well-produced promotional literature and will pick up a great deal of information from the folded A4 sheet they hold in their hands.

When a really original use of the same old 2-fold A4 format arrives it send shivers of pleasure down one's spine.

Your leaflet is about you. Someone who has a way with words will produce convincing prose; an art therapist may fill a full-colour brochure with startling paintings. However, your skill needs to channelled in the right way. A wordy leaflet may make convincing reading and miss the people you are aiming your workshop at. To repeat, marketing is about getting yourself across to the people who want you, so it is no good trying to 'sell' a product that you think people want if you cannot produce it authentically. 'You' and your work should be stamped on everything you do including all your promotional devices. This is why it is difficult to write a leaflet for someone else. That said, a few tricks of the trade do no-one any harm so let us look at what makes leaflets effective as sales tools.

Starting with a format

Before you start writing or designing a leaflet, create a format or structure for your leaflet by aiming to express the *key quality* that your potential clients are going to go for. Here are some examples.

Business Executives: Expensive paper, state-of-the-art typeface, well-designed. Your qualifications and experience clearly stated, not too much to read, repeated message, what it will do for them, how much time it will save them, how it will make more effective at what they do already. NEW! Smart colour ink. What other business execs have said about you and your method. 'Free lunch' (or equivalent, such as a discount on your book). Apply QUICKLY. Limited places. Discount for group bookings.

Key quality: leadership

Depressed women: gentle brochure, soft colours, friendly typeface, written with empathy, a hopeful message, a fair amount to read (to provide time to consider and decide) some sort of organisational requirement - such as a form to fill in. Very clearly structured layout, your personal experience and qualifications.

Key qualities: light and hope

New Age Seekers: recycled paper, U.S.-style layout and typeface, metaphysical symbols, stately impressive prose, quotes from spiritual masters, an impression of mystique, mysteries to be solved, solutions to be found, the Cosmic connectedness of all things. Promise of a safe adventure guided by an experienced guru (for men: active Wise Man symbol, for women: receptive Wise Woman symbol).

Key quality: profundity

Other professionals: prose more important than design, paper etc. Must offer learning, support, greater self-knowledge and fun, techniques for unwinding, possible networking, a photo of you, who you are (not just your qualifications, etc).

Key quality: companionship

Newcomers: familiar, authoritative typeface, not too many words, easy-to-learn techniques, familiar terminology, such as 'assertion', 'stress', 'better relationships'. Promise of a follow-up (e.g., evening or group), questions, e.g. 'Have you ever felt...?' Slightly directive tone, as in a cut-off date.

Key quality: we know you're special

Intelligentsia: slightly wacky, artistic, creative-looking with small, jazzy visuals. Plenty of street cred., not too much prose about meaning or feelings, more about challenges. Stimulate curiosity. Whet the appetite. Offer plenty of breaks (for coffee and chats). Spiky, bare, refined prose - allow them to read between the lines, insert their own subtext. High fees. The fact that you rarely do workshops (etc).

Key quality to express: sensuality

Design - the 'look' of your leaflet

You will save money if you can write and design your own leaflet, though it may take you two or three tries to get it right. Start with the skill you feel most confident in, the look of it, or the words, or the concept, or the colour. If you have already 'designed' a workshop, for example, you already have the basis for the leaflet.

If you don't feel confident about designing, ask someone to help you. A student on a design course, perhaps, or someone else you know who has done a leaflet you like. There is so much scope, even with one colour: textures, screens, layout, photos or illustrations and attractive typography give the impression of colour and interest. Typography is quite an art. To understand it, and its psychological impact, look at books or newspapers and monitor your reaction to the different types and layouts used.

Remember to put function before design. The content of the leaflet and the priority of ideas expressed take precedence over fancy designs.

If your practice involves the use of equipment, do not show a picture of the equipment by itself, e.g. a massage table, an ear candle or tarot card. Show them being used. The picture should demonstrate the therapy. Show someone being massaged, someone being treated with an ear candle, a tarot reader giving a reading.

Keep in mind that the purpose is to get across who you are,what you do and that you can meet the needs of your clients. Visuals help. A photograph of you on the front page depends on how you feel about your image. A short cut, in design terms, is to use symbols (which go straight to the unconscious). Try to avoid initials or acronyms, however decorative, as these have completely different meanings in different industries. (Ask a doctor what 'PR' means, for example). In any case, they tend to get a little absurd. I could, for example, invent a revolutionary type of therapy called TFT. All it would mean is 'The Falloon Technique' which means nothing at all.

If you are only aiming your work at other professionals, the subject (e.g. of your workshop) or your name is more important than design. For a training course, the content, eventual qualifications, expertise of tutors and whether the course is recognised or not (by whoever recognises courses these days) is more important than typography and illustrations. If it is the only course in the country of its kind, you *might* be able to get away with a photocopied piece of typed paper. Though if you are trying to get course recognition, you will just look amateurish and won't be taken seriously. Too elaborate and too complex a leaflet, beautifully typeset and designed, can actually work against you. If it looks costly, your potential students will wonder how much of their fees have gone on the cost of the leaflet. They are after all learning what you teach, not learning leaflet design.

Design includes the positioning of the type (text) as well as the size of the title wording. Thing to bear in mind are where the leaflet is likely to be displayed, such as on a table or a rack or both. Might it also be used as a poster? Or is it simply going to be mailed to an enquirer? A leaflet displayed in a rack with dozens of others has to have impact, and the title wording has to be large. The shape of the leaflet comes into this too: most have two folds to be able to fit into ordinary foolscap envelope. The folds can be the usual 'window' fold, or a zig-zag, known, oddly, as a 'gatefold'. Leaflets that double as posters can only carry printing on one side, and may need to be printed upright (i.e. portrait style) or sideways (i.e. landscape style). To decide which you would prefer, pop round to your nearest community or natural health centre and see what works best. If it is likely to be slotted into a rack, then only the top of the leaflet will show, so make sure your heading is at the top so that it is not obscured by other leaflets.

All your leaflets should be coded so that when people reply to them you know in which mailout they came from. Assuming there is an order form on the leaflet for the respondent to fill in then use 'scratch' coding. It's easy and will not cost you any extra. It works this way. On the original artwork, in small type, put the letters of the alphabet at the bottom of the order form i.e. ABCDE... etc. When you give the copy to the printer ask him/her to scratch off a letter at every 1,000 (say) leaflets printed. When printing, the printer will scratch off a letter of the alphabet on the plates he/she uses, so that every thousand will end with a different letter. The printer should not charge you any extra for this service. One thousand of your leaflets will have the letters of the alphabet ending in 'Z', the next thousand will end in 'Y' etc. This will enable you to monitor the response from each mailout.

My preference for a leaflet which is also a poster is to print on one side only, A4 portrait, and leaving gaps in the text for the two folds, and a wide margin so that the headline text can be inserted at the top, sideways for racks, and other details such as public transport and access can be printed in small type at the bottom.

Second leaflets sent to enquirers can be folded once, resulting in an A5 shaped mini-booklet. You can fit in more information, print on both sides, and the layout is easier to do. There is enough to print a small booking form (at the bottom of the inside right-hand page) and on the reverse of this you can put a code in to monitor where the replies come from. Of course you will need to send these in C5 (to take A5 size) envelopes.

One of the most effective leaflets I've seen, for a series of seminars, was printed, on both sides, landscape, with two folds. The paper was slightly glossy. The inside 'spread' contained the text and plenty of black and white photographs of happy participants at previous workshops (presumably with their permission).

The most artistic one I've seen used a rough, probably hand-made paper with clever graphics and abstract textured patterns. The problem was that it was difficult to read the black printed text on the beige-brown paper, though the effect was so startlingly creative it was worth peering at the text under a bright light. This was for a creativity workshop.

The most typographically-artistic one seen of late is a training course prospectus, which looked as if it took many hours working out how to fit the details of each course in the smallest possible space. Tints were used, to make the paper look grey in certain places. Some of the type was reversed out, that is, white on black or white on grey, and the was plenty of blank space. The leaflet, or rather booklet, looked as if it has cost several thousand pounds. The courses were expensive, there was lots of jargon, and a tempting centre spread detailing residential workshops.

Design also includes the colour of the paper you choose. There are only so many colours of photocopying paper available, though everyone seems to want to use green, pink or white paper and, occasionally, yellow or orange. Black type on sunshine yellow paper is the easiest to read and the colours recommended for people who are visually impaired. There is a limited range of papers used by cheap printers which look good with black type on them. It costs more to used coloured inks as these can only be printed, not photocopied, and only on certain types of heavier paper which costs more.

I doubt, however, that it is cost that causes this sameyness amongst leaflets in our business. I suspect it is more about the lack of design and typography skills. Some of the leaflets, bearing in mind how important they are, look like hurriedly put together afterthoughts, which is unforgiveable. I agree there is a limited number of ways in which a piece of A4 paper can be folded. I agree that leaflets which look too 'posey' can put off certain people. However leaflets which look tatty put off people too. Some leaflets look deliberately down-market in order not to appear elitist, as if they are saying, 'We don't know how to do this either, but we've managed to get a leaflet together so maybe we're a little ahead of you.'

I cringe when I look at my old leaflets. Awful hand-written heading, reduced typed body copy, squiggles and sketchy drawings, uneven printing. I imagine that the recipients suspected that I hadn't done many workshops, and felt tenderly towards me. Or, who knows, perhaps felt superior to me. I imagine they came, though in sixes and sevens, because the content of the workshop was original. I now know that I would have had a higher number of participants if I had taken a little more care. Not being at all 'visual' myself I had forgotten the all important visual/symbolic impact, so my leaflets only 'spoke' to people who were used to seeing typed things with hand-written headlines.

What I believe led to the Tatty Leaflet Syndrome was that in the early days, there was barely any choice about types of photcopying paper, and few therapists understood typography, leaving the printers to do their best. Another attraction of photocopying was, and still is, that you could do it yourself and you only needed to produce one copy at a time, though each looked greyer than the last.

Design is also about who your target clients are. Leaflets aimed at visual people should be artistic and use colour. This does not have to mean expensive four-colour printing. It can mean clever use of textures, screens, reversals and the many other graphic techniques used to produce interesting effects. For instance, if you want to hold a workshops titled 'Don't throw your life away', you could photograph/photocopy/laserprint/bromide a large sheet of crumpled-up paper, and overlay the type on it -

Please, *always* screen photographs. Your printer will explain to you the screening process. They look dreadful and blotchy if you don't, and sometimes print as smudgy meaningless grey areas.

To make your leaflet appear more colourful use coloured paper and contrasting or complementary inks for the printing. Unless you can only afford photocopying, you are not limited to black type.

Use the part of the leaflet that is already there for you, the space, as an essential part of the design. This gives an interesting 'look' and provides gaps in the text to give the reader pause for thought and instil his or her own ideas.

Typography

If experiments in colour are not possible, and you don't feel able to play with textures or screens, then you will need to be fairly imaginative with that other great visual essential, the typefaces.

Typefaces define the style of each letter and numeral. Some of these have embedded themselves in the collective unconscious and become logos, or symbols, like that used for Coca Cola or Harrods, and established newspaper typefaces like Times Roman. When choosing typefaces, designers say that they always look at the S - if it is even, the rest of the type will be too. For those interested, this book is typeset in a typeface called Baskerville. Headings are done in News Gothic.

It takes skill to use a mixture of typefaces effectively. One golden rule is never to use more than two typefaces in the one leaflet. Most books and many magazines obey this rule. Magazines like ID are the exception. One typeface is often enough. Use Sans Serif typefaces for the headings, Serif for the main body of the text. Sans Serif is type without the squiggly bits. Serif types have sqiggly bits. Stay with familiar typefaces and don't choose fancy typefaces as they distract.

Printers will show you a book of the typefaces they have available, as will desktop publishing bureaux.

Don't make the typeface too small. Your eyesight may be good, but many people in this country wear glasses and if they have to put their glasses on to read your leaflet, you are effectively putting an obstruction in their way. If they are required to fill in an order form, allow enough space to put in their details without squinting.

Illustrations

Symbols, logos, photographs...anything to stimulate the imagination and connect to your potential clients makes for a more effective leaflet. A logo, incidentally, is a mixture of typeface and design, like a trademark.

A colleague who holds 'Goddess' workshops includes sketches of well known Goddesses in her leaflets. I Ching symbols are effective for certain clients. You can draw your own mandala, bird, animal or fairy-tale figure. Beware of obvious symbols. For instance, there are quite a few phoenixes and Ying-Yang symbols about. Obviously it is best to choose a symbol that relates to your work, otherwise it may confuse the reader.

If all of this is a mystery to you, and you plan to be in business for some years, it is worth hiring a designer who can create a 'look' for you. Use can then use a format which you can follow for all your promotional literature for years to come.

Writing leaflet copy

This is perhaps the most difficult task. Finding the words that will effectively sell what you do is not easy. Thinking up that one line that says it all, is probably the most time consuming task. Advertising agencies got paid lots of money to come up with the lines 'Probably the best lager in the world' and 'it's the real thing'.

Whatever your leaflet is promoting, it is important to say this first of all and describe it without including too much jargon. If you are not confident about writing, practice by taping yourself describing the therapy to a real, or imaginary, client. Better still, to a telephone caller, as the people who read your leaflet won't be able to see you.

It's best to stress the benefits of the therapy rather than go into length describing the therapy itself.

Make ways of paying easy: cheque, credit card, cash, switchcard, phoning through and paying by credit card, postal order. The less obstacles you put in the way of them paying you the better.

Stress the uniqueness of your therapy and the way you work.

Bear in mind that your leaflet is also your sales brochure. The way it is written and designed should 'lead' the potential client through the text to the booking form, and by the time they are there, they should have their cheque book ready to send off the deposit, or be poised over the telephone ready to dial your number.

The leaflet needs to state who you are and what you do, how the person will benefit. Think about when, why, what, where and how. A telephone number where you can be contacted is essential.

There should also be a small biography of you. At least, until you are famous.

Checklist of Essential Contents

- What your therapy is
- Where it's happening (especially if this is different from the booking address)
- When (date, opening times, how often, etc)

- Your name. Large if you're famous, small if you're not
- What your therapy does and how it works (or is applied)
- Whether it is new/popular/well-established
- Surprisingly good things about it, or what its different about your way of doing it
- What it will do for clients
- What sort of people gain from it
- How many people are coming (if it's a workshop)
- What can be learned from it or if it has a recognised certificate
- How much it costs and if there are discounts or concessions
- Who created it or how it developed
- Your qualifications and training
- Testimonials (if relevant)
- How you benefitted from it yourself (if relevant)
- Advantages of where you work
- Punch line
- How to book (cut out booking form, though this will mean VAT on the printing cost)
- Final date for deposit receipt/booking
- Your telephone number, address, fax number (if you have one) *separate from the booking form*

How to address resistance

In your writing, you will need to break through any resistance, which is usually based on fear, and address every objection the reader may have about becoming a client. The way to work out what these resistances are likely to be is from a history of previous objections. In acupuncture for instance clients may have been concerned about whether the needles hurt and whether they might catch anything from them. So you should emphasise the painlessness of the process and the fact that all your needles are sterilised, or that every client gets their own set. You might even use a 'question and answer' format.

Nutritionists could avoid the fear a client may have of a complete diet change by explaining that any changes would be introduced gradually. Anyone new to body work, be it structural integration, Alexander Technique, Shiatsu or Polarity Therapy will want reassurance that the practitioner is fully qualified, that only muscles are worked on, and that all movements are gentle.

Group facilitators know that on-going groups go through predictable stages. The first is usually about people feeling unsafe in the group. Subtly acknowledge these concerns and offer a safe and supportive environment. An obvious way to do this is to emphasise your experience in working with groups. If you think shy participants are fearful they won't get a word in edgeways then say that everyone will be given time to speak. A non-specific way of saying this is to limit the number of group members. Clarity about boundaries is also a good idea.

As people unsure about groups like to think they may meet people similar to themselves, you could offer interviews, or a free open evening, or some other way of making sure the members will be compatible. This applies more to groups dealing with specific issues such as eating disorders or addiction recovery. You will need to make it clear what stage of recovery, for instance, the group will be working with.

The main objection to weekend workshops is that they take up the entire weekend, and some take up the Friday evening as well. Emphasise that you workshop is well worth going to, well worth getting up for, a special event in their lives. Try and predict what your client group would most want to do at the weekend and put this in the literature. e.g. Have a break, Be entertained, Learn something, Get comfort and attention, Relax, Be vigorous, Make new friends, Start a whole new phase of their lives, Provide them something to take away, Provide a change in the routine, Provide respite from a crisis-ridden home life.

Agree it may be hard work (remember the work ethic!) and that they'll feel better at the end of it. If the sole purpose of your workshops is to get more clients for individual therapy, then it should be an introduction to the type of therapy that you do.

Depending on where you are working, you may need to give details about accomodation, nearby shops and eateries, quiet rooms and, if you are using a natural health centre, whether there will be a chance for a few hours off for a massage or a float in the centre (booked in advance, of course).

The crucial words

In every leaflet, there is one sentence (also known as the punch line) which finally converts the reader into a client. Here are some examples.

- FREE - all welcome
- see yourself floating effortlessly, free from the effects of gravity
- only good people get depressed
- with skilled guidance, it is possible to release both present and past life traumas
- people return home feeling secure, centred and with a new direction
- at the end of the course, you will be a fully certified practitioner
- How do you know you can't heal?
- In 36 hours anyone can learn to give a full-body shiatsu
- Depression within a sick society may be a sign of health
- an elegant, efficient and subtle system of mind training
- learn practical and enjoyable self-help techniques based on your natural abilities

Printing

How Many to Print

Mass mailshots are, I believe, a colossal waste of paper, money and everything else, particularly for workshops, groups, and therapies. The big banks regularly mail out insurance flyers with statements.

The response rates are likely to be very low to these flyers and hence deserve the title 'junk mail'.

Why do some people print 20,000 leaflets, have exactly the same number of people at a similar workshop as someone who printed 3,000 leaflets? There are many reasons for this and any form of promotion that you do has to be cost-effective. The main reason is targetting. The more you reach the people who you know want your service, the greater the response you will have. Always try to get in an appropriate mailing. Quality of the leaflet is another important factor. Does the content and style of the leaflet address the needs of the respondents?

Leaflets can be sent through the post or stacked in racks with everybody else's. My experience is that those taken up from carefully targetted list are more effective than those sent 'cold' by mail. Though direct mail is a more personal way of reaching people, its effectiveness very much depends on who is on the mailing list, how up-to-date it is, what else is in the mailing, and what other promotion you are doing.

If you are aiming at more than one market you will need a choice of leaflets. If nobody responds to the first one, you may need a new one. Trial and error is important.

If you are promoting a single event: one workshop, a centre open day, or a short course, then 3,000 leaflets, carefully targetted, will be enough, and *if* you are offering something unusual and in demand. If it is amazingly unusual, and you get it to the right people, you might only need 200 leaflets.

If you have plenty of time and are one of those well-organised people who know what they are doing a year from now, try a *leaflet campaign.* This works well if what you are doing is new to you, or if you need more than a hundred people, or of you need a small number of people paying huge fees.

Operate on a basis of getting a 1% response rate to your leaflets. If you need to get 12 responses, you will need to print 1,200 leaflets. If you are photocopying the leaflets you can do them in batches of 400, so that if you reach your target quickly you won't over print.

Consider printing three types of leaflet. (1) a leaflet which is an introduction to what you do. This flyer should be cheap to print and you can put out virtually anywhere. It contains basic information (2) a leaflet for each event or service, or series of events. These are likely to be updated regulary (3) a leaflet which describes all of the services you offer. This should be glossier, not date sensitive and mailed out to those who are already clients and those who are likely to become clients.

Printing

It is well worth shopping around for printing. A day, or even two days, telephoning local printers will pay you dividends. Independent local printers often charge less than High Street franchise shops. Look in your local directory for printers offering short-run prices. Ask the local authority training centre if there is a print shop. Find the cheapest quote you can, and get the printers to compete with each other. Haggling pays. If you also need the printer to do your typesetting, choose one with a computer on the premises. Printers located outside of cities are cheaper. Try *Exchange and Mart* to find them.

Money can be saved if you are using coloured ink by waiting until the printer has another job using the same colours. Packs of A4 paper are purchased by printers in reams, so if you want a special colour or texture, you will have to pay for the whole ream (500 sheets). For a small run, photocopying usually works out cheaper (except for the VAT) though you are of course restricted to black print.

For a large run (over 1000) printing is much cheaper than photocopying. The more you order, the cheaper per copy it is, as the main expense is in setting up the presses and making the plates. People who know their way around printers, and can guarantee them regular work (such as quarterly newsletters) can negotiate truly rock-bottom prices, such as £120 for 10,000. The reason for this is that the printer can use bigger sheets of paper for larger volumes of work, and so save on machine time by doubling up. Most local printers and franchises only print on A4 (the size of a sheet of typing or photocopy paper). If you compare the price of leaflet printing to, say, a 36-page booklet which might cost only £1,000 for 2,000 copies, you can see how expensive A4 printing is by comparison.

If you only print your phone number, the printing will carry no VAT. If it has a form to fill in, it will carry VAT. Do not ask me why. You may need to remind your printer of this especially if they are primarily doing photocopying, which always carries VAT.

Paper comes in a limitless variety of colours, weights, coatings and textures. All printers have sample books of special papers. The lighter weight the paper, the more opaque it will be. There are probably 200 varieties of 'white', so if you are asking for samples, ask for something that has already been printed, otherwise you may be landed with several thousand beautiful leaflets with the print on the reverse side showing through. Photocopies vary - some producing greyish copies, others miraculously producing improved clarity. Printers talk about weights of paper in gsm (grammes per square metre). 80 gsm paper is the average photocopying paper.

Paper has different 'finishes'. 'Matt' paper is the type always used for photocopying and comes in different colours. 'Coated' paper (also referred to as 'art' paper) is glossy. It is often used if there are photos in the leaflet. It's harder to print on than matt paper too. Printing can be done on matt paper or coated paper.

If you want consistency in your print, ask the printer what kinds of plates they use. Some last longer than others. Metal plates are the most expensive and the best quality; there are also plastic and paper plates. The printer will advise you which is the best sort to use for the number of copies you want. Some paper plates can last up to 10,000 copies, so for most leaflets, metal plates are an unecessary expense.

Other things you need to know about are artwork costs. The printer will give you a price for 'camera-ready' artwork, that is, artwork which is the same size as you want it to appear, with nothing to be done to it. If you want photographs inserted, overlays, reverse outs or anything other than a straightforward copy, the printer will give you an artwork preparation quote. If you provide flat black and white artwork, and you want the headlines and other sections printed in a different colour (known as 'spot' colour) the printer will need to make 'separations' and there's another charge for these.

You can save a little by doing your own 'separations'; that is, two separate pieces of artwork, one of them perhaps on an overlay (you need a special sheet for this). The additional cost is because the printer may not have a camera on the premises, and has to send all the platemaking to another firm.

Of course, if you know someone who has access to a DTP computer, your artwork (and typesetting) problems are solved.

....and other ephemera

The idea of ephemera is to add originality to your event and to make the participants feel special (which, of course, they are) and wanted.

Obviously whatever you choose has to relate to your event/ workshop/therapy, and be appropriate for your target client group. You wouldn't send nice little nonsenses to business executives, for instance, unless perhaps it was a particular sort of pen, tie-pin/scarf-pin. Go back to the Seven Needs list for a moment. Do your chosen clients want something they can touch, handle, enjoy, think is clever, makes them feel good? Something beautiful? That is why they are coming to see you, is it not?

You can make little ephemeric things to send to your final applicants, especially if it's a workshop. You could spray plant essences onto each piece of paper, for instance. Enclose mini-packs of 3 healing incense sticks, or pressed flowers or leaves, or tiny shells, tiny gemstones, or anything you fancy - a bit of Origami, if you are so inclined. A self-recorded short tape, even. 'On this weekend, you will be doing some meditative exercises. If you have never meditated before, this tape will guide you through this most simple of relaxation and centering techniques'. I sent some people (small) packets of Kleenex with my Therapists' Fun Book, which caused a certain amount of hilarity. There are dozens of card packs around now. You can send a different one to each enquirer. 'This is your personal Angel Card. This is key word for you to think about before you come to the workshop.' You then have the perfect ice-breaker - everyone can say what they felt about receiving their card, and whether the word meant anything to them. If you are asking clients to bring along drawings of themselves, you could enclose tiny Christmas-Cracker sized packs of coloured felt pens.

You can send specially-made 'invitations', and if it is a larger event - a seminar, open lecture, fund-raiser - it is worth having individual lapel badges made.

I have mentioned elsewhere the example of a former lollipop lady sending cut-out lollipop-shaped cards to people (for an Inner Child workshop). If you think this sort of thing is in totally bad taste you won't have got this far down the page, anyway. I don't think there is any harm in a little fun, or giving people little presents if they are going to give up a weekend of their time to an event which to them (even if not to you) is going to be personal and memorable.

There is upmarket ephemera and downmarket ephemera. Pieces of healing bark would be considered upmarket, silly badges downmarket. A bag of herbal tea (to ensure a good night's sleep and an interesting dream the night before) would be upmarket. I think if you are promising light and joy, hologram badges and even rainbow stickers (though they are getting a bit tacky now) wouldn't go amiss.

It really depends upon how solemn you are, and how solemn and shockable your potential clients might be. They may be put off by what they may perceive as 'frivolity'. I haven't yet been to a workshop at which crystals or pink roses were distributed to departing participants, or anything to 'link' them all together. I have been to workshops where I felt pressured to buy something before I left. Actually, I have never been to a workshop which offered me my money back if I wasn't satisfied.

Now there would be an innovation

Leaflet Distribution

There are many ways that you can distribute your leaflet. Be sure that whichever way you choose you make sure that the leaflet are likely to reach your potential clients. A typical expected response rate is 1%. So if you want 10 clients for a group you will need to print and distribute 1000 leaflets. The response rate is very dependent on how well targetted the mailing is, as well as the design of the leaflet.

The Brainwave Marketing Book carries lists of New Age organisations that have mailing lists.

- Distribute at holistic fairs. You may be able to find a representation service that will display your leaflet. Otherwise contact the festival organisers to find out who will be there and contact them to see if they can display your leaflets on their stall.
- Put in with mail out of magazine.
- Put in with mail to a target group. (direct mail)
- Door to door distribution. This can be haphazard.
- Co-operate with another practitioner to go our in your shared mailing to reduce costs.
- Mail out to your own database of old, and existing clients, and referal agencies.
- Leave at a wholefood or similar shop. Make sure you have the permission of the owner.

Advertising

Advertising is the most expensive form of publicity, and, not surprisingly, requires the least effort from you. This is because the primary purpose of all the 'promotional' media is to sit there longing for you (and in many cases actively persuading you) to advertise with them. They earn their living by doing the circulating of the information for you (well, that's one way of looking at it). There are several different sorts of advertising, most of which are known as 'space'. Advertising is also grouped into 'above the line' and 'below the line', which basically means expensive or cheap (in that order).There are several different types of advertising in widely varying media. For most practitioners, advertising doesn't work very well unless it is in a directory, a quarterly, or in the type of publication people keep for several months. It works best for people who have no other outlet, such as mail-order companies.

Sensible advertising

The purpose of advertising is to draw the attention of as wide a market as possible. The more people you reach, the more expensive your marketing will be. For practitioners, the amount of advertising you buy, and the media you choose, needs therefore to be very selective. A single advertisement has no purpose at all unless it is part of a co-ordinated campaign or for a one-off event - such as advertising in the local paper for your open day, or for your centre or service in a supplement on complementary therapies.

Advertising is a tax-deductible expense, even so it is quite a large expense. If you need to advertise, you can economise by haggling with your chosen paper, especially late on a Friday or on the 'deadline' day, when they might have spaces to fill and you could negotiate a discount. They may become fed up with you if you do this every week, however. Some publications offer discounts in any case for regulars.

If you are considering long-term press advertising, ring up a variety of publications and ask for their *rate cards.* These will give you some valuable information, such as detailed readership profiles (ages, social groups, interests, other purchases) and usually a free copy of the publication. The one time that press (also called display) advertising is cheaper than anything else is if you have something you want to sell by mail-order. A quarter page advertisement (for instance) will cost you vastly less than an insert of your leaflet or order form; it will also stay in the magazine a lot longer. Although it may seem unfair that quarterlies charge the same rates as monthlies for a smaller circulation, they are usually read only by a 'special' readership, so you know who you are dealing with - and they stay around for three or more months in readers' homes.

If your clients come by word of mouth you don't need to advertise. Advertising does not, in any case, only mean space in a publication - there are several options. The factors to consider, regardless of your chosen medium are (1) size of market reached (readership or people attending a fair, for instance) (2) value for money (3) other regular advertisers. If in the 'personal' section of your local paper's classified pages there are 100 similar therapists advertising, there is no point you becoming Number 101.

Advertising in specialist magazines is wiser than in listings weeklies or local papers, unless you are fairly certain of the readership. Your answermachine will be full of 'pest' calls and time-wasting enquiries, including those by some keen phone salesperson trying to sell you diaries, insurance policies, voucher booklets, double glazing, or plumbing services. Also, of course, by the classified advertising manager trying to sell you more classified advertising.

Wording

Before wording your advertisement, you may need to check with your professional association or training centre about any limits on statements you can make about yourself. It is unlikely that you will be permitted to put '...probably the best herbalist in the world'. Your creativity is therefore going to be frustrated. Never mind - you can use it elsewhere. In your leaflets, perhaps.

In any advertisement (as with other forms of publicity), you will need to make it clear what you are offering, how much it costs, where you are, how you can be reached, and the times you are available. The simplest way to test an advertisement is to look at ones you responded to yourself, and work out why they grabbed your attention. Use the AIDA technique as advocated in the section on 'Why leaflets are so important'. Adverts should grab attention, arouse interest, stimulate desire and then spur to action.

I mentioned earlier how symbols are the best form of marketing, as they go straight to the collective unconscious; words (especially onomatopoeia ones like 'crunch' or 'smooth') and concepts are part of symbolism - we may learn and understand new ways of thinking, but it takes a generation or more for these ideas to reach the collective unconscious.

As well as knowing about your client's personality and lifestyle, you will also need to know what goes on in her unconscious, as this frequently bears no relation at all to her external appearance or apparent character.

Below are some examples of advertising messages from Big Business which zoom straight to the collective unconscious. All advertising (including what you don't say) has subliminal messages, because everyone who has ever written a line of advertising 'copy' will tell you that they have agonised their way through all the marketing processes I have written about, and many more, to achieve one punchy 'selling' line. (That is why they are paid such vast sums of money). If what I mean is not clear, take five minutes to review how the following copy lines effect you: 'I'll bet he drinks Carling Black Label'. 'Go to work on an egg'. 'Australians don't give a XXXX for anything else.' 'Every car you'll ever want'. 'We won't make a problem out of a crisis'.

Different types of advertising

Classified advertising is the cheapest, and consists of a few lines in the back of the publication under a heading. The publications will do the typesetting for you, and they usually have 'box' rates or 'semi-display' rates to make your advertisement distinct from the rest.

Display advertising is a much larger space, costing much more, and you have some choice, though not always, about where in the publication it will appear, such as on an editorial page, or grouped in sections with other display advertising. A display advertisement can be typeset for you, if you trust the publication to do it the way you want it. It is usually preferable to provide your own 'artwork' as this will make your advertisement look the same as all your other promotional literature.

Much of what is covered in the section on leaflets can be applied to display advertising, including typefaces, design etc. Some other things to be aware of are as follows. Choose the appropriate publication i.e. the readership are most akin to the type of client you are trying to reach. Look at the publication you intend to advertise in and see how the adverts are laid out. Make your advert different in some way, so that it will stand out from the others. If possible ask the publisher to position the advert next to relevant editorial. Failing that ask to be positioned on the right hand page and nearer the top, as this tends to get read first. The biggest mistake is to try to cram in too much text at the expense of not giving the heading enough space to grab the readers' attention. The next most common mistake is to use the business name as the heading. The heading is meant to grab attention, so make it do that.

You will generally be trying to reach clients in your own locale. Thus advertising in national magazines and papers means that much of the readership will not be relevant. However, if the publication has a specialist bias, such as *Human Potential*, which is aimed at people who have an interest in psychotherapy, the response may be better than advertising in a local current affairs newspaper. It's best if you can find a publication that is distributed only in your locale *and* is also a specialist publication in your field. Holistic London, for instance, covers New Age in the London area . A list of specialist magazines, complete with advertising details can be gleaned from *The Brainwave Marketing Book.*

You could also produce your advertisement in the form of an *insert* (a single sheet or a leaflet) which the magazine will put into each copy. This is more striking, as your insert will fall out. The downside of this is that many retailers shake out any leaflets before they put them in the racks. The reason for this is that the leaflets fall out when customers are thumbing through them and they leave a mess on the floor. So it's often best if you put an insert in a magazine to ask that they only put it in those that are mailed out to subscribers. This way you can be sure of not wasting any.

You have to print and despatch possibly thousands of inserts at your own expense, and the rate of including them is much higher than a display space. There is a limit to how many inserts one magazine can accept per mailing. Some publications will only include inserts in mailed copies as opposed to newsagent's copies, and only the very high-profile magazines will have specially bound supplements. One or two big circulation magazines can organise separate batches, so that your leaflets only goes to a certain area. However, for the purposes of this book, and bearing in mind the relatively small circulations of most of the specialist publications, this may prove too expensive for most advertisers.

Merchandise is a form of advertising which you also earn money from, though many people give merchandise away. It can be something as simple as a bookmark with your, or your centre's, name and address printed on it; a carrier bag for people to take away from your stall at a fair or open day, a T-shirt advertising your astrology service or massage training school, a 'limited edition' or 'collector's item' of some sort, a kite, a fan, or souvenirs such as matchbooks, blocks of memo pads, biros, and anything else you can think of. A book or tape of your workshop could also come under that heading if it encourages people to come to your *next* workshop. Now that city centre photocopying shops sometimes have machines which can enlarge a passport-sized colour photo and print it onto a T-shirt, having what you do emblazoned on your chest becomes a serious possibility. Only you can decide whether something like this is worth the cost and the trouble. My feeling is that such frivolous items add to your appeal at the big holistic and health fairs, especially if there is some sort of slogan which would provide the user with a little cachet, you know, 'I Survived An All-Night Float'. If you don't know any T-shirt printers (usually silk screen printers) look in the classified sections of promotion business magazines such as *Campaign*.

Point of sale: This is usually a poster or streamer, or even a balloon, in the window of the centre where you work, or where your workshop is going to be; or if it is a product, in the shop window or inside the shop. There are rather a lot of posters and notices in natural health centres these days, so yours need to be fairly eye-catching to make any sort of impression. Some options are mobiles, special offer vouchers, competitions, and complete window displays, a polystyrene cut-out of you in full swing with a pile of your latest books and tapes artistically arranged around your feet.

TV and radio: This is known as 'airtime'.

On the whole, a variety of advertising and publicity works best. People who receive, say, your leaflet in a direct mail shot may think 'I have heard about this somewhere', without quite realising that they saw a notice about in the local health food shop that morning.

Advertising for a one-off event, a workshops, say, is very different from continuous advertising to promote yourself or your centre. Advertising should always be for a reason, as it is virtually useless if there is no purpose behind it other than 'getting my name known'.

The most effective form of advertising is the 'stepped' campaign, i.e. one that is spread out over some months in advance of your event, using a mixture of different types of advertising, and publicity, in different media. Obviously this costs a lot of money, and it depends on what you are doing. Once everyone has heard of your event, it becomes an annual fixture, so you won't have to work so hard, as people will expect to hear about it at the right time of the year.

Getting on the Radio

It is much easier to get on the radio that you think. For practitioners, local radio is especially good, because it will broadcast to the area you practice in. Local radio work on small budgets and are very welcoming of items of interest that are topical and which costs them little money.

The *Brainwave Marketing Book* from Brainwave lists radio stations in the UK, complete with phone numbers and address, and with details of whether they have programmes sympathetic to health and the New Age.

The first step is to listen to your radio. Get an idea of the programmes and the nature of the programmes. Then send a News Release to the station/s. A news release is similar to a press release, so look under the section 'How To Get Your Name in the Papers' for how to compile one. Then follow up your news release with a phone call. Or you could try simply phoning first and finding out what programmes they broadcast which may be relevant and listening to that show. Find out the name of the presenter and ring or write to him/her.

If you want tuition in handling radio interviews then contact Carrie Bates. She is a practitioner herself who has worked for many years in radio. She runs workshops and individual sessions for practitioners who wish to use the radio. See the Resource Section at the back of this book for how to contact her.

When you are asked for an interview here are some points to remember to do before the interview:

- Ask what the first question will be
- Write down three things you want to get across
- Make sure the listeners are left with some way of making contact with you.
- Find out if it's live or recorded
- Ask if you can have a recorded tape of the interview.
- If it is pre-recorded ask how much of the interview they will use

- Find out the context of the interview
- Listen to the programme on your radio to become aquainted with the presenter and context of the programme
- Work out some questions you would like to be asked. If you are asked these questions then you can make the most of the opportunity.
- Think of questions you would not like to be asked and rehearse some answers to them.
- Find out who the programme is broadcast to - the type of people it is aimed at.

Some hints and tips for the interview

- Give yourself enough time to get there
- The stations work on a low budget so don't be suprised if there is no one to greet you and lead you through and hold your hand. Because the stations are so preoccupied it may seem unfriendly and hostile. It's not the case. It's just appears that way.
- Wear clothes you feel comfortable in. The listeners can't see you so it's not important how you appear.
- Ask what the first question will be.
- Have a good anecdote or story to tell
- You may be asked strange questions. This is because the presenter is not familiar with the subject as you are.

Taking Phone Calls

Responding to initial enquiries

Some general rules in responding to phone calls are as follows :

- If possible get the person's name and address and phone number and send them a leaflet
- Make follow up calls if you say you will get back to them. Evenings and weekends are probably best for getting back to domestic calls and it's also cheaper then.
- It's cheaper and quicker to phone rather than write a letter
- Some callers are put off when they find your line is constantly engaged. If you use the telephone a lot then take advantage of BT's Call Waiting Service. If someone is trying to ring you and you are already on the phone, you will hear a tone, and you are able, by pressing certain keys on your phone to switch between conversations. It is not an expensive service.
- Treat each phone call with as much respect as those you make. Don't have an attitude of 'Oh no, not another phone call, who's bothering me now'.
- Keep a notepad by the phone and put as much of the conversation on to the pad as possible.
- Be polite and listen to people's complaints sympathetically
- Keep your records within easy reach of your phone.
- Try out different ways of relating on the phone.
- Ask the caller whether it is possible for them to talk confidentially. They may be phoning from work and may be reluctant to go into details about their problems if the call is likely to be overheard.
- A well rehearsed script can be useful to answer standard questions you may be likely to be asked.
- Make sure to listen to the callers needs and respond to them. Stress the benefits of what you offer.

- Learn not to take rejection personally.
- Answer the phone immediately
- If you can only answer the phone yourself between certain times because you are seeing clients at other times, then put the times you are available to take calls on your brochures. You should have an anwerphone to take calls at other times, or better still a person who can handle the calls and take messages.
- If you have someone else taking messages for you then brief them fully on how to handle your potential clients over the phone. Ask them to get the caller's phone number if possible and you should ring them back as soon as you can.
- Don't be tempted to answer the phone when you are with a client. It makes the client feel abandoned and they resent their session, that they are paying for, being used for somebody else.

Answerphone

Answerphone messages should be brief, so as not to put off callers. Some callers do not like to leave messages, so provide a time when they can speak to you in person. Ask for their phone number in the message, so you can get back to them, and then get back to them quickly. Keep a check that your message is not becoming distorted as time goes by, by phoning your number occasionaly and listening to the message.

Typical message

This is (071) 444 4444, Joe Bloggs speaking. I am sorry there is no one to take your call at present. However, if you leave your name and phone number and the best time to call you, I will get back to you as soon as possible. If you wish to receive a free brochure of the workshops/individual therapy I offer then please leave your name and address, together with your phone number if you wish. If you want to speak to me in person I am available in the mornings between 10-11am or afternoons between 4-5pm. Thank you for calling.

How to Get Your Name in the Papers

Other people writing or talking about what you are doing to the public (i.e. your potential clients) is called publicity. This includes leaflets and other forms of print which announce, or make known widely, who you are and what you are doing. It is about your relationship with your public. It is an activity, and is *often* called outreach.

Publicity, being a general term, can include articles in the press about you, a listing in a personal growth magazine diary page, or a poster that someone else has put up for you in their centre. Publicity includes knowing how to get your name in the papers. Confusingly, material that you send to, say, 200 bookshops about your latest publications is called 'retail promotion'. Although you have to pay for printing and postage, publicity is usually free.

Everyone knows the power of the press. First of all, clients think you are famous because the local rag has written you up. More important, clients think you must be very good at what you do to have got yourself noticed by a busy, important journalist. And to some people, all journalists are important, some more than others, so members of the press (or, as one should, say the media) are important influencers of potential clients.

Much of the time, the popular press attacks natural therapies and I don't think this matters very much. Journalists, who can become a little egotistical because everyone thinks they are so important and clever, tend to underestimate their readers. So even if they write as 'shock horror probe scandal' story about you, somebody out there will say 'Oh, great, I've been wondering if anyone round here did polarity therapy with electronic crystals' and there you are with 20 new clients. As they say in Hollywood, *All Publicity Is Good Publicity*, and it's true. Even terrible publicity can be good news if you can successfully sue the newspaper for libel. Unless, of course if you actually *really did* the terrible things they say you did. We only need one disaster to affect the credibility of an entire profession.

If you are planning a career as a self-publicist, be prepared to be infuriated much of the time. You may, for years, have been trying to get someone to write about the effects on health of suppressing feelings, for instance. Then one day the reporter writes exactly what you've said, only it is attributed to a doctor at a stress management clinic in Harley Street. It's less depressing to forget those writers who only believe what doctors say and concentrate on finding willing ears.

So start small, with achievable objectives.

Once you decide to give it a go, bear in mind that different approaches are required for different results. Are you aiming for specialist, general, or trade publications? There are often different writers to be contacted for a general mention of you in relevant articles, or news stories about your new workshop/idea/product. It is highly unlikely that writers will come to you unless they have already heard of you, so you need to know where to find them and how to approach them, as well as what their interests are - what is likely to 'grab' them, and what their attitude will be to what you tell them. Despite the famous journalistic objectivity there is actually no such thing, though there is, among professionals, balanced reporting. In any case, journalists are only human and they come in all varieties.

How do you get hold of journalists? Newspapers and magazines with large circulations have staff writers as well as freelancers, so your first contact would be the editor of your chosen section. Personal growth writers on the smaller circulation monthlies or quarterlies are usually unpaid, and many of them are therapists. The *Brainwave Marketing Book* lists specialist publications and jounalists covering the New Age field.

A good place to start is a publications which deals with your type of work, probably a professional journal or specialist magazine. The journalists most likely to be interested in hearing from you are freelancers, who earn all or part of their living by selling news stories and/or articles (features) to professional and consumer magazines, national and local newspapers, and in some cases, to radio or television stations. Some also write and research books, or programmes, and some write publicity material, such as brochures and reports. Many writers are also therapists. Some writers will write about anything, others classify themselves as 'health and fitness' specialists. Others only write about psychotherapy subjects, and there is the occasional 'medical' reporter who braves it and writes surveys on alternative therapies, sometimes being so bold as to actually mention osteopathy or, even more riskily, homeopathy. It is often the 'health and beauty' reporters who write about massage and aromatherapy, as it still has an indulgent image. If you want to win a journalist's heart, throw sex into your story somewhere.

Some of these writers may be 'the authority' on their subject, so they will always be looking for something new to write about, especially those who edit their paper's section (usually a local paper) on holistic health or natural therapies. Though many freelance writers have regular columns in one or more publications, others sell their work from scratch, or suggest features to editors so they tend to be interested in 'newsy', saleable information from practitioners.

The term 'journalist' usually means someone who writes about what other people are doing, while 'writer' gives the impression of someone creative. All journalists are creative writers, and may use other names for their different writing styles or subjects. The two terms are, therefore, interchangeable, and to save repetition 'publication' can also mean 'programme' and 'printing' mean 'broadcast'.

If you don't actually want to be a writer yourself, then the purpose of getting your name in the papers is, of course, to get more clients. Before you even think about publicity, be very clear about why you want it. In other words use the same approach as you do to writing your leaflets. Be single-minded about this, or it won't work.

First rule of Getting Your Name In The Papers: *think about what the readers want to read.*

And don't be discouraged by failure. Keep trying, journalists need you too!

Co-operating with freelance journalists.

Holistic therapists have a great deal in common with freelance writers. Both professions require the development of left and right-brain abilities. All are self-motivating, imaginative, need to keep up with trends, find gaps in the market, continue learning, think conceptually as well as logically, apply theories to practice, and reach highly individual 'end users'.

Building up relationships with writers therefore holds few mysteries. We can help each other to sell our services and to promote holistic therapies in general. An understanding of the workings of the media is important for a successful publicity campaign. Freelancers are our channel to the media as well as to the public. Recognising that the healing profession is as much of a rat race as any other is a first step.

The advantage of contacting specialist writers (for instance those listed in the *Brainwave Marketing Book*) is that they will be interested in your work and will know what you are talking about. They will also know how to apply your information to other topics or current issues you may not yet be aware of. There are specialities within specialities. For instance, if a journalist writes about healing you should determine the audience he/she is writing for. Does he/she only write about healers with famous, or even Royal, clients? Or does he/she write about professional matters, such as accreditation or training? It is reasonable to phone and ask these questions, and to ask which newspapers/magazines the journalist writes for, or is hoping to write for. Find out if the journalist writes regular reports of who is doing what? Or would he/she want clients' before and after stories? Which of them should you contact? Regular readers of professional publications and health sections of newspapers and magazines will know which writers specialise in which subjects, and which of them follow trends. Media watchers will also have an idea of which publications are dedicated to 'quack-busting'. Some publications exist to list everything that is happening, with little or no follow-up or authentication, and really want you to buy advertising space. Others do in-depth reports, well-researched, and with well-known people quoted. Those new to the publicity business, staring doubtfully at lists of names, may be wondering where to start, of whether to start at all. Bear in mind that we all need each other. The question is who needs what, how much of it, and when?

Before you start

If you have never done any publicity before, it is best to start in a small way, with realistic targets. It makes sense to approach a publication or a writer who specialises in your field.

Before contacting anyone there are some points to consider, and, once you have started, some general rules to follow.

Though most of the following refers to publications, it is always worth contacting your local radio stations. You could even suggest programmes or phone-in topics.

Among the many questions you need to ask yourself are: what are you hoping to achieve? Do you want a short news item, or a long article going into your therapy in depth, or a serious feature about a treatment or supplement, with research data and client stories? A tongue-in-cheek 'filler'? An advertising supplement (a local newspaper standby)? Which readership do you want to reach? Other professionals? Potential clients and patients? Young people? The local community? The Single Market? Parents? Sportspeople?

Focussing on these points will make your selection process easier, and save money on unnecessary mailings. It would also prevent your story being misused. As one therapist commented, 'I don't want to find my serious talk on self-hypnosis headlined: *'How to increase your bust size by willpower - picture'*

If your event is local, the national newspapers will not be interested unless they are running a series on the subject, and, of course they rarely tell us this. However, national journalists follow up stories from local newspapers, so that is not necessarily the end of it. Keep an eye on the 'personal' classified ads; programme researchers sometimes advertise for candidates for 'topic' programmes.

The warm-up

Before contacting a freelance journalist, be aware of the possibility that only reason they want to be listed in directories is to attract the attention of editors who will commission work from them. It is a good idea, therefore, to make friendly contact, explain what you are doing, and ask if the journalist would be interested. If he/she says a firm 'No' then give up. If you are sending out a press release (see section below) you could telephone first and say that it is on the way. This will personalise your white envelope when it arrives (preferably first class).

These are the first steps in building up a relationship, however temporary, and, as with any other type of alliance, journalists will phone you back (a) if you arouse their curiosity and (b) if they feel that they like you. If what you are doing seems news-worthy and, more to the point, saleable, even better. However, it is always worth building up contacts for the future. Journalists have a vast store of general knowledge and constantly accumulate 'background' information.

If you feel comfortable using the telephone, and answerphones hold no fears for you, leave a message for the journalist, giving as much detail as there is time for, and a cut-off date for a return call. An introduction, a message that more information is on the way, and a time when you can be reached is helpful. If your call is returned ask the journalist if this is simply information-gathering, or whether it is a telephone interview, in which case you will not want to say anything that you would not like to see printed. The journalist may ask if you have a press release, photograph, brochure or tape inlay card, for instance. If you don't, then you could write a letter explaining what you do. If the journalist does not seem interested, or is too busy to talk for long, it is worth asking what other information is needed, or whether it is better to meet, or for the journalist to sample your product or therapy, or attend a seminar or media reception (if you are having one).

Approaching magazines direct

Journalists and editors on the smaller natural health magazines are friendly and accessible, and always interested in new therapies or ways of working, particularly the professional magazines. The consumer specialist magazine writers vary. One advantage of going to the big London fairs is that these publishers often take stands, and you can meet the editor or news editor, and probably the advertisment sales manager and introduce yourself and your work.

They will willingly tell you what sort of supplements they are planning in coming issues, and give you guidance on when and how to send them information.

If you do not have the opportunity to go to the fairs, the best place to start is the specialist magazine which you read yourself, as you will already know the writing style, the names of writers reporting in your field, and what features they have run over the previous year or so. When making your first telephone call, you will be able to say 'I've noticed you're interested in diets for allergies. I'm a cranial osteopath and I've developed a technique for relieving hay fever and sinusitis, and I'm studying breathing techniques for asthmatics' (for instance). If you don't feel comfortable using the telephone you can of course say this in a letter. The other thing you will know about the magazines you read yourself is how up-to-date they are with the news. If they seem to be lagging behind the others, perhaps because of their long lead times, you will also need to think ahead and tell them what you will be doing six or nine months from now. As you do with your clients, all you need to do with writers is to think about what *they* need, and you can't go wrong. Don't be discouraged if they already know all about it, or someone else is already doing it. Try contacting another magazine which may not know about it yet.

National newspaper journalists are difficult to contact. They are often out, usually busy (perhaps the sole health writer trying to deal with a huge subject) and if they don't know you they will only talk to you if you talk to them in journalese. That is, start with a grabby 'headline' and go on from there. 'Hallo, I'm a specialist in addiction recovery. I was wondering if you knew that there's a new American technique combining hypnotherapy with herbal medicine which assists the withdrawal process.' Offering 'exclusives' doesn't work any more. What can work quite well is if your subject is being reported somewhere else, perhaps in a professional monthly. Then you can say 'There's a piece in a medical journal due out in two weeks' time about midwives using acupuncture. Would you be interested in another angle on the story?'

As you've noticed, there is jargon to be learned here. On daily papers, articles are usually called features, and news items are stories. There are also news features. Often either can be called a *piece*, and things in the gossip column or 'news in brief' columns are called *items*. It helps if you know the way your chosen newspaper works. For instance, if the health writer only writes about allopathic medical breakthroughs or NHS re-organisation or house surgeons' overtime, try the features section which deals with family, home, or 'life' subjects. Specialities are very narrow on large-circulation newspapers or magazines, and if you get through to the wrong person they will probably have no idea what you are talking about.

This is why it is easier, and far less demoralising, to start small and with a publications you know. If you do have some information which is likely to stop the presses, and really is a scoop, contact a freelance who will be most appreciative, as he or she can sell three or four different versions of your story to different papers and probably radio as well.

Timing

If your event, launch or opening clashes with another important diary date, change it. The festival *Here's Health 1990* clashed with Wimbledon Finals week, so there was little space in the papers for anything else. The *1992 Health Show* clashed with the Glastonbury Festival, the EuroPride Festival and National Music Day.)

If you are launching yourself or your product at one of the many holistic fairs, you will have let the press know about you well in advance. If this sort of timing is unimportant for you, it is useful to remember that at certain times of the year, less advertising sales mean that papers and magazines have more editorial space. The 'silly' seasons, summer and mid-December, are good times to try and place an offbeat story.

Deadlines

All publications and programmes have editorial 'copy' (written material) dates, which are spread throughout the week/month/quarter/year prior to printing/broadcast. 'June' magazines are on sale in May and prepared in April. A local paper on sale on Fridays will have finalised its feature content at least one week before that. Advertising supplements may have been scheduled at the beginning of the financial year. Some of the glossy consumer 'health' magazines have six-month lead times. Listings magazines always state the final 'copy' date, and information should be sent ahead of this, though not too early. The glossy women's magazines work several months in advance and, in the case of food sections, a year in advance in order to photograph produce in season.

Some 'news' stories in daily papers, for instance in the 'health' sections, have been decided on and written two to three weeks earlier (and the idea quite probably suggested by a freelancer who knew a certain DHSS report would be available that week.) Approaching staff writers on newspapers is a demoralising experience, because they will not phone back if they don't know who you are, unless you make your message intriguing enough. At certain times of the day, as the writers approach their own deadlines, they will not even take down your name. Approaching a freelancer is, therefore, somewhat easier. And do contact them before your general mail-shot.

Press release

A Press Release is a means of telling a carefully-selected number of journalists what you are doing in a professional way in a format which they will recognise.

They are efficient looking basic information sheets, on A4 headed paper, with newsy 'headlines' which give a clear 'what, when, who, where, how and why' summary of what is happening. One sheet is enough, as journalists receive dozens of these every week (on national newspapers, hundreds).

To make your press release stand out from all the others, you may need to create a 'press pack'. Colour, style, a little imagination, humour, and attractive visuals, all presented in a handy folder are, of course expensive, so you need to decide what value you place upon yourself/your product and the impression you want to give. Visuals could be an activity photograph, a before-and-after photograph or drawings, a wrapper, inlay card or sample (if relevant), a short biography of you (and/or back-up research data), client testimonials, some background material and press cuttings, about you or your therapy. A workshop leaflet on its own is not enough;

you will need to explain the significance of what you are doing and its application.

Media lists

Freelance journalists, health and other relevant magazines, radio stations and newspaper section editors are listed in *The Brainwave Marketing Book*. In addition, Brainwave will sell you up-to-date media packs with printed labels. If you want to go into press relations in a big way, a company called *PR Newslink* produced regularly updated books, called *Editors,* which are automatically sent to you if you are subscriber. The press cuttings agencies will also send you lists of publications they 'cut' (a good way of obtaining a free press lists!) However, this is never the end of it, as staff move around, or change their specialities, or, indeed, are made redundant, quicker than you can say 'scoop'. So, unfortunately, you will need to update your list, or at least check out a selection of important names every time you send out a press release. If you cannot face doing this, always add, after the person's name, their job title so that if they have departed someone else will open the envelope. You will in any case discover who has left when you do your follow-up phone calls. This can be extremely embarrasing if the supposed recipient of your missive left a year ago.

Nevertheless, you can maintain a small, manageable press and promotion list merely by reading your chosen magazines regularly.

How to Package a Story

When you contact a journalist, whether by phone, press release, or letter, how can you 'sell' your story? Why should anyone want to write about you? The answer is to use the same techniques as journalists do in order to sell theirs.

Can you tip off a journalist about something you heard of at a meeting or conference in exchange for a 'mention' of what you are doing? Is there some topicality, a tie-in date, which you can use as a 'hook' on which to hang a story? Can you 'wrap' a straightforward event; for instance the opening of your centre, into a saleable story? Was there local opposition? A row about planning regulations? Are you the first local employer to use a new job-creation scheme? Are any of your practitioners famous for something, or make tapes, or write books or give lectures?

Is yours the fifth identical story the journalist has heard that week? If so, why are there five new stress centres in your town? Is it the capital of stress-related depression? Is it something in the water? A national scandal? Is the American authoress of a book about the very subject you have been teaching for years appearing on the Wogan Show next month? Are you the neighbourhood phobia specialist? Could you 'hit back' at something on the radio/TV/last week's paper? Editors, though rarely writers, love 'hit back' or 'row' stories.

Prior to a transport strike, could all your staff arrange to be photographed on tandems? What can you offer to the most harassed and deprived members of your local community? Some of these ideas may appear flippant, however, many editors underestimate their readers, and if the end result is that your message gets across and your therapy/product is publicised, where is the harm?

If you are promoting a new therapy, could you create an image for it as well as creating a name? Just as an example, could you follow aromatherapy, which seems to have entered the nation's consciousness as divine-decadence-made-respectable without the tricky word 'massage' ever being mentioned?

Holistic therapists can benefit by applying their best skill, their 'client-centred' approach, to their own publicity.

Being ahead of the rest

It is a serious blow to non-competitive holistic practitioners to realise that there is an undignified scramble going on out there. However, there is no need to actually compete. Everyone's best asset is their individuality. You don't have to be (or pretend to be) the best/newest/first in your field. You only have to be you.

Trust the process. You may be ahead of your time and suddenly realise that the outside world is ready to hear about you. This is the green light. If you want to be a little more cynical, there is no harm in that either. By this I mean the 'amazing' discovery, following 'years of research' that all living things need light to thrive. One day soon, anti-biotic manufacturers will 'discover' the benefits of the common onion, just as American allopathic cancer researchers are now 'testing' South American herbs and roots. If you can start your press release with 'Thousands of arthritis sufferers have been duped into buying a costly new drug while a carrot a day has the same effect....' (I'm making that up) you will probably receive a return phone call from every health writer in the country. All it takes is imagination and application.

And remember the personal touch. Many a cynical hack has been converted by the experience of a free session of a particular therapy or attendance at a growth workshop. If you feel purist about 'bribery' think of this as a 'review'. And however tempting it may be, avoid jargon and initials. That said, an appealing new word for an old therapy has results; how many people have heard of 'rebirthing', though would not read an article on Reichian body therapy? And who has not heard of Royal Jelly and Evening Primrose Oil?

Bear in mind which expressions and terms are acceptable to the average non-specialist publications. Social workers are now referred to as 'counsellors' in many news stories about disasters, because social workers have been much maligned in the press as horrible people who take children away from their 'innocent' parents and are blamed for numerous social ills. Wearying as it is, the tabloids still refer to depression as a 'mental illness' or talk about 'nervous breakdowns'. However, they have made concepts such 'stress' well understood. If you watch television, listen to the radio or read newspapers, you will know which words are used often enough for you to be sure your press release (for instance) will be read and understood.

The follow-up

If your efforts are met with silence, you could either send a follow-up press release, or letter, or telephone again. The journalist may simply be not interested, or too busy with other things, or the press release may have been lost in the post, or may have arrived after the journalist's deadline. This is why it is wise to contact as many writers as possible. Especially if you have a dated event. It is, of course, disappointing to find that something very important to you, or to your organisation, is of no interest to the media. It is even more frustrating to be told that had the news arrived a week earlier, it would have been very welcome.

Getting Mentioned

There are several ways of getting your name in the papers apart from all the hard work of Press Releases, phoning round, following up and worrying about it. Here are some ideas:

- saying something controversial
- doing a stunt, being famous for something else (e.g. a book)
- discovering a cure for something
- being the only person in the world doing what you are doing
- offering something free or cheap for a limited period only
- being new/the first in your area/a prize-winner of something/a prize-giver of something
- doing a charity run (etc).
- Being a dial-a-quote person. For this you have to be well-known enough and accepted as a professional spokesperson in your chosen field. For instance in Well-Woman Week, you may be the osteopath or nutritionist the health editors phone for a quote about the value of your therapy for pre-menstrual tension, natural childbirth, the menopause and preventing osteoporosis.
- You can become a local star by being a survivor of the particular illness/disease/experience the feature is about, you know - 'Polarity Therapist Returns From Arctic', 'Acupuncturist Wins Boxing Trophy' 'Crystal Healer Finds Diamonds in Bromley'.
- Being relevant. This means ringing up a particular columnist on a paper (local or otherwise) because what you offer is something of particular interest to their readers. (Newspaper sections are usually: health, women's, money, lifestyle, sociology, education, travel, entertainment, children's, and where to go.) Your phone calls may need to be followed up by a Press Release, letter, or an information

pack, plus invitation, sample, or review copy. And you must tell the columnist well in advance, and tell her/him again nearer the time, especially if what you do is dated.

- Being listed in your professional association directory. Certain outreach-minded associations regularly tell newspaper section editors what they are up to. The British Psychological Society is, appropriately, superb at this. The result being that whenever there is a story about someone famous that is covered everywhere, and the journalists wants another 'angle', they ring the Society for a contact name. By this method, a previously-obscure arts psychology practitioner was not only quoted, but also got commissoned to write a psychological appraisal of Prince Charles' paintings. Next time you are writing to your association newsletter, suggest that a little PR would benefit everyone (primarily you, of course.)

Motto: self-promotion begins at home!

Now you are a fully-qualified publicist.

Workshops

To fill a workshop there are three basic guidelines (1) provide what your clients need (2) address their resistances (3) promote it adequately and with good timing. It also makes sense to cost the workshop, because even through you fill it, you may not make a profit unless you've done your sums.

It is important to do a few quick sums and see what is most cost-effective for you. Bear in mind that if you do a variety of work, some of the participants may do further workshops or become individual clients and an estimate of this should be reflected in the costings. It may be that your workshops are not intended to be self supporting, and serve only as an introduction to catch clients for individual work or future workshops. Some workshops (for example, at the big fairs) are to tempt people to come to a later weekend workshop.

Basic rules for a successful workshop

The reason that people want to come to workshops is because they want to learn, primarily about themselves, and people learn by various means including sensing (listening, seeing, touching), experimenting, experiencing, observing, analysing, creating and sharing. They enjoy the companionship of people like themselves who they may never have to see again, the chance to express feelings in a supportive environment, the opportunity for finding solutions to problems, and the possibility of exciting life changes. And there are as many other individual reasons for going to workshops as there are human beings. The factor they most have in common is the preparedness to try something new and to take risks.

Andrew Ferguson, who runs workshops at the *Breakthrough Centre* for people who want to run workshops, advises the following basic rules:

- Never cancel
- Don't offer too much too soon
- Flaunt your specialness
- Make your workshop an irresistable priority
- Pick a good time

- Get people committed
- Start planning it about a year to nine months ahead
- Address any objections or resistance in your literature
- Offer confidence. Emphasise that you are worth it, and so are they
- Tell people what it will do for them, the benefits of attending

Why people don't come to workshops

Being in a group can be scary for many people. People often have a bad memory of being in groups, or of groups, stretching way back to their childhood. The may have been bullied in school by gangs. They may have not been selected by the football team. They may have been scapegoated by their classmates. Having a group turn on you can be a very frightening experience. People often fear that the group will not accept them. They fear that the group won't like them: the way they dress, the way they talk etc. They will imagine they will have to do things they don't want to do. For example they may think they will be required to give a speech and fear that they may be ridiculed. You must, to some extent, allay these fears. You can do this by putting in your publicity that you aim to provide a safe setting where they will be accepted; that they will be protected and cared for. If participants do feel safe in your workshops then they are likely to find it a pleasant experience and to go to further workshops and recommend their friends to go. For further information on addressing resistance see *How To Address Resistance* under the section in this book on *Leaflets.*

It has to be said that some workshops are quite dreadful and off-putting, and many people have had alarming experiences. You need to offer safety in your literature, plus experience and plaudits from previous participants. If you have never done workshop before, keep your target clients small, twelve at most. Keep it simple and don't try and deal with too many issues at once.

Make sure the impression you give will stay with them. Make it clear that you know all the reasons why they might hesitate to make the appointment/send off the deposit and that's 0K, and then *give them positive solutions to all those objections.* If you can achieve this, then they will recognise that you, and you alone, can give them positive solutions for lots of other things as well. The worse thing that passengers can be told on an airplane is 'don't panic'. These words have the opposite effect. A much better phrase is 'please remain seated and relaxed'. The moral here is to stress the positive and not to mention the negative. Do not, for instance, in your promotional literature say that the workshop will not be scary experience. Instead emphasise that it will be a safe group.

Another reason people don't come is that you told them about it much too far in advance, or much to close to the date. Aim to avoid the season periods when participants are unlikely to do workshops. These times are immediately before the summer holidays, just after the summer holidays, and leading up to Christmas and January. Think carefully before holding a workshop on a Bank Holiday weekend, unless you are in a city and only targetting out-of-town clients and can offer access to reasonable accomodation. A course is less risky than a personal growth workshop in holiday periods. Those quiet times can work the opposite way if you are holding a country residential, an alternative to Christmas (since so many people hate it or don't celebrate it for religious or cultural reasons) or an exciting week-long New Year warmer-upper.

You might be offering a stale, unoriginal workshop that nobody wants to come to. Or your literature may be unconvincing; perhaps the message is not clear, or you are not demonstrating enough confidence in yourself or valuing of your potential clients. If you don't come across as confident and competent, people will not feel safe with you. The chapter on leaflets goes into details and will help you to avoid the pitfalls of presentation.

The obvious reason people don't come is because they haven't heard about it. As well as advance publicity, planning, content and timing, successful workshops need a little extra promotion as there are so many of them. You are not really competing, because what you are offering is unique, so you need to make sure your promotional style is unique as well. The simplest way to do this is to make it an expression of you. And remember that the best leaflet in the world has to go to the right places, the ones where your potential clients are.

The magic formula

Your magic formula is whatever it is about you that is unique. It may be a new way of solving an old problem, or an application of an old technique to a new problem. If you are in tune with the times and a step ahead of other people doing the same sort of work as you, you will have recognised a mood and a need and tailor your workshop accordingly. The mood of the nineties is self-empowerment; the need is, as always, for healing, and most urgently now, healing the Planet. The combination means individual responsibility - we can no longer trust those in authority take responsibility for us. Co-operation is replacing hierarchies and power no longer means control, it means valuing individual strengths.

Look back and identify the most successful thing - not necessarily a workshop or even a therapy, you've ever done, and work out why it was successful. It may be that it was beginners' luck. You had great self-confidence and it did not occur to you that no-one would come; or that you really are unique; that the workshop had a friendly atmosphere because you knew some of them/some of them knew each other; you did not offer something you couldn't do; what you offered was authentic, and in tune with the needs of the time; you had just written a best-selling book or been on TV and everyone had heard of you; you reduced the 'risk factors' in spending the whole weekend with total strangers. They could learn something they needed to learn, and you were the only person in the country who could teach it, since you were the person who experienced the unique process which healed your own wounds.

How to be a famous workshop leader

You need to be very good at, and famous for, one thing and one thing only. Also you need to continually and widely advertise the coming year's workshop. Have sample tapes, for instance, available by mail-order at a low price, particularly if what you are offering is a hearing or sound-producing experience. Or if not a tape, some kind 'taster', especially if your fees are high, and they will need to be, to pay for all this promotion.

As I have said elsewhere, the most famous people are those who are the best known. Many are merely famous for being famous, excellent at self-promotion, or because they buy an awful lot of advertising space, and write books and give talks and turn up determinedly at every single holistic fair. They have also got themselves interviewed somewhere, so that they can enclose cuttings with their leaflets, or reproduce them in their brochures, or they have had their workshop previewed.

What's special about your chosen venue?

An important selling point about workshops is where they are held, and this needs to be detailed on your brochure. What are the advantages of the venue you have chosen; that it is in the wilds; that it is minutes from the City centre, the theatres and restaurants; that it is near a beach; that there is a cafe or a laundromat in the building; that it is in an established centre where people know good workshops are held; that it is in a sound-proof basement in a brand-new conversion; that it is fully accessible; that there is ample parking space; that it is near public transport; that it is in the middle of one of London's most beautiful parks; that it is within two minutes walk of the Whirly-Gig disco or the Barefoot Boogie?

Remember that yours is never the only workshop on the subject (even though your presentation of the subject is unique). Someone extremely lazy who does not have a car and goes to a lot of workshops will go to those which are within easy reach of their home by public transport. Other people will want to know how near the cafe or pub is, or a park where they can wander, or a market where they can do their shopping on a Saturday, or indeed a Sunday. You never know which small bit of information will help tip the scales in your favour (well, you *do* know if you have targetted them accurately). Put in as much information as you can without making it look like a tourist brochure

Making them come

Getting people to come to workshops is about demonstrating that you can meet their needs and reducing fears they may have about attending. The basic idea of a workshop, and the original meaning of the word, is that the participants go back to their usual lives armed with a new portfolio of skills. I personally would never go to a workshops which promised 'simple' techniques - I want something challenging. Others may feel threatened by challenge, and prefer simplicity and modesty in their workshop leaders. I'd like to feel that I will be enabled to learn how to develop so-far dormant qualities using my existing abilities.

In the chapter on Research, you will find detailed descriptions of what influences people, how they make choices, and what needs they have. To make people come to your workshop you have to demonstrate to your target client group that you can either meet their needs or show them how meet their own. If you identify your target client as closely as possible, you will be able to include in your literature the punch line which is, *them,* the deciding factor.

Example for Setting Up a Series of Workshops

This example is based on a series of workshops set up and ran by a therapist who is not named here.
Therapist profile: a former teacher with a wide general knowledge and experience in different types of therapies for a range of problems. Committed to the holistic approach and frustrated with 'guru' types. Dislikes workshops because of the risk, effort and planning and choice of too many of the same sort of workshops; likes giving talks about therapy; does training and supervision with professionals.

Overwhelming public image: professional confidence.
Purpose: to earn money
Title: to be decided
Concept: Self-help skills
Target clients: Women
Image: Holistic, empowering, informal, safe.
Venue: New holistic centre in busy suburb. Excellent public transport, road parking, access.
Timing: Early summer, following Mind Body Spirit Festival.
Promotion budget: £500
Revenue required: £2,000
Maximum participants: 20
Number of facilitators: 1
Materials: Flip chart, markers, reference books, cushions, paper and crayons
Practical work: leaflets, advertising artwork, mailing lists, support services, identify and arrange other promotion and publicity, notes for workshops, book extra supervision session, prepare small stationary, comps slips, booking confirmation slips, envelopes, stamps, etc.

Preparatory work
(Two months in advance)

Purpose: Self-explanatory

Concept

The concept of offering a workshop teaching self-help skills came up as the result of *research* which showed that (a) the best-selling books in three key personal-growth bookshops all dealt with recovery, especially the 12-step method. (b) The self-help skills books available at the time, apart from the 'recovery' worksbooks, were sparse (only three) written some years ago, and none included the Whole Person approach.

Requests for self-help studies funded by local authorities carried out in Oxford and Leeds showed that most self-help groups were concerned with (1) Community issues, e.g. neighbourhood action groups, and (2) problems; tranquilliser addiction, bereavement, illnesses and disabilities, carer support, and ex-mental health system patients' rehabilitation. Other research showed that in general, social work (which is primarily concerned with families) has no tradition in running groups despite the fact that every social work client lives in a group of some sort, a family or community. The *gap in the market* therefore appeared to be for training people in self-help skills which they could pass on to others if they wanted to. In addition, they would have experience of being in a *group* and the dynamics could be fed back to them at the end of the workshop.

The research also showed that the largest numbers of self-help groups in the UK are set up for, and by people, who want to recover from addictions and eating disorders, and for adults survivors of childhood abuse; either sexual abuse or the emotional abuse resulting from being the child of an addicted parent (e.g. to alcohol). Every one of these groups is run on the American-originated 12-steps process.

What needed to be different about this self-help skills workshop, apart from it using the Whole Person (holistic) approach ? It would need to be:

- Practical and straightforwardly presented
- Problem-oriented
- Reasonably priced
- Women-only (because of nature of problems dealt with)
- Small group for safety of participants, and to allow time for individual attention

- Not a 12-step group
- Informal
- Well-structured
- Not a weekend.

Why not a weekend? First, because there are too many problems to be dealt with in one weekend, and many participants would feel cheated. Secondly, because self-help skills need to be practised from week to week. Thirdly, because women not feeling they have a particular problem (e.g. addiction) might avoid the whole weekend because of that. Fourthly, to have a 'group experience' requires a separate process, which would also take several weeks to explore.

Probably the main reason was the facilitator's confidence in giving talks, and dislike of weekend workshops. Further additions to the concept were added during the promotion period. The working concept therefore was:

A self-help group for women, offering a practical guide to holistic skills, held on one evening a week over the summer months (12 weeks) with at least two of the evenings concentrating on explaining holistic jargon and the Whole Person (in this case, Whole Woman) approach.

Target Clients

'Women' was obviously not a specific enough description for the target clients. Without more details, it would not be possible to reach them. The women who would most benefit from this type of workshop are: age 23-plus, working or with income, free one evening a week, with an interest in and limited knowledge of the holistic way of living, a wish to help themselves and serious health and emotional problems. These women may or may not be single, and interested in if not committed to feminism. They have probably never been on a workshop before, though may have learned yoga or meditation and tried aromatherapy, for example. They have probably avoided attending women's groups before. They are reluctant to completely give up allopathic medicine and have some preparedness to work on themselves, a reasonable level of self-awarness and a good deal of courage. They will be intelligent, and have come from either strict or hostile backgrounds, in other words, experienced limits to their self-expression as children. They will be rather unnassertive, though respond better to leadership than authority, and refuse to be patronised. Having put up with a lot, they now *know* there must be more in life!

Image

The key qualities to express were: healing, light, cleansing, hope, straightforwardness, safety, communication, learning, understanding, and companionship.

All this had to be expressed without actually stating it all. The first and most important choice to make was, obviously, the colour of the leaflet. This came up in a visualisation, though could quite easily have been the result of a brainstorm session. The obvious feeling for most of the key qualities is flowing pure water. Since a stream is a little slow and shallow, a better image was a waterfall, which is also powerful and, in case anyone has forgotten, generates electricity and negative ions. The leaflet, therefore, had to be aqua, and the print a similar, though obviously darker colour. The paper with its own mottled effect, proved too expensive, so in the end a plain aqua paper was chosen. It was decided to have the leaflet as a single-sheet A4 upright, for budget purposes as well as for the 'upright' image of a waterfall. Another advanatge of this colour was that though it was green, it was a very different green from the one everybody else seemed to be using for their leaflets, therefore it would stand out.

When the leaflet was printed, someone said the colour was a North American Indian colour for 'speaking your own truth', which was rather nice. The facilitator rushed round the local charity shops and bought several tops in matching shades of green and wore them from then on, thereby appearing to be cool, calm, and connected.

The title became *Healing the Whole Woman: A practical guide to holistic self-help.* The wording for the leaflet, which had to fit the image, had to explain exactly what would happen and avoid, though recognise, New Age jargon, with a phrase such as 'despite the New Age jargon, holistic self help is.....'.

Necessary alterations and silly mistakes

It was reluctantly agreed to keep the group open (open meaning that new people could come throughout the series). First, because some women would want to come to only two or three of the workshops and secondly, because it offered the chance of more women coming to later workshops once the word had spread at how good it was.

One difficulty was timing. It had to be held in the evenings as people who could afford to pay would mostly be working. For it to take place in the summer months (so that participants could arrive and leave in the daylight, and there was less chance of having to battle through grim weather) it could only run for eight weeks, until mid-July, because of holidays. The dates chosen were from after the second May Bank Holiday to mid-July. Unfortunately, the first workshop fell in the middle of most schools' half-term, something not thought about at the planning stage. And that, combined with it being in a Bank Holiday week, meant that lots of people were away. This was not desperate, though, as it started immediately after the *Mind Body and Spirit* exhibition. People who had picked the leaflet up there were very much in the holistic mood and came along out of interest. Several then signed up for the entire workshop series.

Venue

The aesthetic reasons for choosing the venue were that it had a large, airy, attractive room, with plants everywhere and lots of windows. There were plenty of mats and cushions, a flip chart, music equipment and a friendly and supportive woman owner, who also had considerable experience in running workshops. As the centre was all on one floor and was new, access for wheelchairs was possible. There was a well stocked kitchen area, enough toilets and a small back room that was unlikely to be in use (in case anyone wanted to disappear temporarily). It also had a burglar alarm and a fire exit. There were disadvantages. As it was new, not many people knew about it. However, this became less of a problem on finding out that the centre was holding an open day on the Saturday prior to the first workshop date, which the facilitator was welcome to attend and promote her workshops. In addition, and this was an important asset, workshop leaflets could be included, at a very reasonable rate, in the centre's own open day promotion, which was extensive. Public transport was excellent, there were several nearby cafes, late-night grocery shops, and on-street parking seemed reasonable. Disadvantages: the centre had previously been a small factory and had been deserted for some time. Local teenagers, mostly boys, had got into the habit of throwing stones through the broken windows and jumping on to the flat roof. If the rear room was going to be in use, this would mean the practitioner, and clients, walking around and using the kithcen area and loos, which would disturb the workshop. However, nothing in life is perfect. It was decided to run the workshops from 6.30 - 8.30 instead of the usual 7.30 start.

Timing

This was not so much choosing the dates, as it had already been decided, for various reason, to hold it in the early summer.

One obvious problem was that the series was planned with only two months notice. This made it too late for listings in the holistic magazines or professional association journals. Had this been planned earlier, the date chosen would have been perfect, because all the quarterlies appear in the two or three weeks prior to the end of May bank holiday. However, this hopeless inefficiency was rationalised away (!!) by agreeing that since it was a local workshop, there was no point promoting it in national publications, and that this would only have been of real value if it was a training course for professionals, in which case, it would have to have been advertised at least 6 months ago. Nevertheless, this was obviously going to be a rush job, and the budget was small. As it would be spread over two months, the late start on advertising would only effect the first two or three workshops, there was still hope of rescuing the situation. There was never at any time the thought of cancelling. The deposit had been paid, and with summer approaching, the next chance of doing the workshop would be mid-September, when no-one has any money.

It was decided to do a specialist mailing of leaflets, advertising in the local weekly, which has a large circulation, a good health section, and a holistic supplement about once a year, and four other publications: a weekly listings magazines, which was promising a health supplement shortly before the workshops, one holistic newspaper, a national newspaper with a good women's page, *The Guardian,* and a women's monthly.

Budget

Since the purpose of this workshop series was to make money, money would have to be spent. However, the facilitator had very little money for promotion, only £500. This meant that a great deal of legwork would have to be done, so plenty of time was allotted for this. The advertising costs for each of the papers chosen would have to be £50 plus VAT, including the cost of preparing the artwork, as the papers all had different column sizes. The first task was to get some quotes for typesetting and printing. A local franchise printing shop offered a ridiculously low-cost job: £25 for typesetting the leaflet and £150 for printing 3,000. Once they saw the leaflet copy, they upped the typesetting price to £150 as well (maybe they suddenly had a lot of orders). This messed up the arrangements, already made for a distributor to take the leaflets around various centres, and of course meant the mailshot had to be delayed by ten days, which was valuable time lost. This also meant most people and centres would receive the leaflets during the week prior to the first May Bank Holiday. Not good. Lesson 1: trust not local printers desperate for work who promise anything just to get you into their shop. Lesson 2: ask everyone you know before you start about good local printers. Luckily, a friend offered to go to a DTP bureau (where you can rent a computer by the hour - as long as you know what you are doing, for a very resonable rate, and prints are inexpensive). The leaflet was typeset and so were all the advertisements, and a printer was found who was willing to stock the aqau paper wanted and to use a special colour ink, and do it as a rush job for no extra charge. 3,000 leaflets cost £110, which we later discovered was expensive, though it was the best quote found.

Why such a small number of leaflets, when 6,000 is the recommended minimum? Mainly because it was a specialist workshop, and there were a limited number of women-only centres in the area where working women went. Secondly, the time, effort and postage costs would have been doubled. Another point was faith in the workshop: no-one else was doing, or had ever done as far as we could establish, anything similar. Because of this, the therapist was certain it would be listed free in various publications. However, to make extra sure, the costs of preparing and sending out a press release had to be added to the budget. In the end, another £100 was added to the budget to cover the distribution costs and inclusion in a mailshot which would be sent out two weeks in advance of the workshop start date. Remember this amount was the *promotion* budget, and did not include costs of renting the venue, fares to and from, materials, tea, milk, juices and nibbles. Nor did it include the costs of the time (friends are wonderful), and this whole business seems to operate on a co-operative basis. However, if you were 'hiring' all this advice and guidance, it would be very expensive, a guestimate of £2,000.

Income

The promotion budget was blown, and the delay to the mailout reduced the chances of filling the hall. The anticipated income for this workshop series was, therefore reduced to £1500. This greatly reduced the expected profit. So things were looking bad.

We could not change the amount the participants were to be charged, which was £10 for an evening. If they attended all evenings we had promised it at a discount price of £65 for the series, and we expected half of them to buy the series.

Finding the Clients

As the target client was very clearly identified, it was easy to work out where she could be found, and also deduce where she was unlikely to go. Meditation produced the awareness that they would be in five well-known places. Ideally, this meant reaching four women from each of these places. Not a very tall order, you might think. Getting this wrong, however, could be a disaster. Four would come from women's centres, four from the *Festival for Mind, Body and Spirit*, four from adverts and listings in magazines, four would come from other well-known people (that is, well-known to them) and four from the holistic therapy world (including practitioners). As you can see, each of those five 'well-known places' is actually open to wide interpretation. Finding the women's centres was easy, there are very few of these. The Festival was also easy, and this involved renting an A4-sized bit of wall at the ever-friendly *Pathways* stand

and borrowing a bit more space on a friend's stand the opposite side of the hall. The Press Office also got papered, not just because the press might drop in there, but because *all* the other publicity-minded therapists and workshops leaders would also go there, if only to see what everyone else was up to. The other choices were to wander around wearing clothes the same colours as the leaflet, and giving leaflets to likely-looking stallholders, plus contacts and friends. Sitting in the bar was also effective. 'Well-known' people would include GPs, hospitals, therapists, friends of theirs, TV and radio personalities. The 'holistic therapy world' includes health food shops, natural health centres, bulletins, other therapists, the venue's open day, especially. This latter category was the least used, as the targeted clients would not automatically go to these places, except, possibly, health food shops and other therapists. To be on the safe side, a few actual 'well-known places' were included: libraries, the local museum, theatre clubs, adult education centres, former training centre.

Publicity

The leaflet: budget restrictions meant that there could be only one piece of literature, as opposed to a leaflet for mailing and displaying and a separate poster. The leaflet therefore had to also be a poster, another reason for it to be A4 upright. The layout was done carefully. For instance having the title up the side (in case the leaflets were displayed), folded, on their ends instead of stacked on a shelf or a table. As they would serve as posters, the title and the date had to be much bigger type than would normally be used on a leaflet. Spaces had to be left in each of the three possible folding places: in the middle (for folding it to A5 for the press) and a third of the way down and two thirds of the way down (for folding it into three for mailing). Since there was quite a lot of information to go on the leaflet, it required some skill in editing the essentials down, and in the event, the spaces proved helpful as they broke up the written material. The order, as always, was: what, where, who, when, how, how much, how to book and any other details. Because of having the lettering up the side it meant there was a wide margin, so tiny public transport and access details were inserted here. In the end, it looked as if the leaflet had been specially designed that way. And though the leaflet would have been considerably cheaper in black and white, or even black on photocopying green, it was worth it to pay the extra for the special colour to help it stand out.

Advertising: The great disadvantage of advertising is, first, that it costs money and, secondly, the small spaces that are affordable mean you can't put much information in. Someone has to be very interested and curious enough to phone up for more details. After a little negotiation, reasonable rates, close to the proposed budget of £50 each advertisement, plus VAT, were established. The listings magazine which was running a health supplement was offering a special rate plus guaranteed free listing, which seemed well worth the cost. In the event, however, there were no bookings from this source. This was because the editor of the supplement, who had obviously been told to pack in as much advertising as possible, told a fib when asked if it would be a holistic supplement - it was more of a keep-fit supplement.

The other con was the local paper. The cheaper rate was in the 'forthcoming attractions' section, and the advertising manager of this section neglected to mention that the following week the paper was running an alternative therapies feature. This fact was also unknown to the health writer who, as a result of considerable PR, actually came along and did an interview, which never appeared. Moral: ask everyone you speak to on a newspaper if anyone else is doing anything they know of that might remotely be of relevance to you, since the staff obviously do not tell each other. In any case, the writers may be freelancers, and no-one ever tells them what is going on.

Other moral: *nothing is free.* The holistic paper chosen said it was too late to post artwork, so the copy was read over the phone and a confirmation leaflet sent in so that the ad manager could check against it the next day.

In the event, three of the listings magazines ran short pieces (longer than the usual listing) in the relevant sections, as was anticipated. However, since these listings appear in the week of the event, people have little time to choose, or change arrangements made in advance. Listings are useful, as people who see your advertisement somewhere might check to see if there are more details than you could fit in your advertisement. In addition, the value of listings is that press cuttings are useful. They can be used to promote further workshop series. It also convinces people you are real. So they are more of value as general PR than advertisements for your workshop. Like everything else, they do not work on their own.

The response from the advertisement in The Guardian (in the Saturday Noticeboard section) was hopeless, only one enquiry. Advertising on or near the women's page, or in the society job pages, usually a good source for specialist workshops, was prohibitively expensive. There were several enquiries from the local newspaper advertisement, and no bookings.

The best response came, as would be expected, from the leaflets. These were picked up at women's centres, a health food shop, the Mind Body and Spirit exhibition, the Pathways Bulletin, the counsellors' network, and a friendly local museum.

Free publicity: leaflets were put up everywhere locally that didn't cost anything: health food shops, libraries, adult education centres, one small museum, hospital out-patients' department, the dentist, and of course the centre where the workshop was being held. Whether they *stayed* up is another matter. The listings would also qualify for this section, except that they were not the result of the leaflet, there was a convincing press release and telephone follow up.

The interview for the local paper, also the result of the press release and a follow-up phone call, would also have qualified, had it appeared. No-one ever gets listed as a result of a leaflet arriving unannounced, all on its own in a plain brown envelope with a second-class stamp on it.

The leaflets were also left at Neal's Yard Agency, a London centre which specialises in displaying leaflets. They earn their money by taking a percentage of any booking they arrange for you. They have since changed the system and you have to pay them rent for displaying your leaflets. In addition, you have to join their network and pay for this, and supply a therapists' profile plus photograph. Unless you have a profile, this takes time to put together. As it happened no bookings came from this centre.

Paid publicity: as with any kind of marketing you have to go to where your clients congregate. You can't leave a pile of leaflets somewhere and assume people will turn up to collect them. More cost-effective, then, is one of the leaflet distribution services. However, for this to work well, you need to give them a minimum of 2,000 leaflets, and preferably 6,000. If you do the same workshop year in and year out, you need to give them at least 6,000 four times a year. You can either leave it to them, or tell them specifically where you want your leaflets to go; in this cases, women's centres, health food shops, adult education centres and theatre clubs or cafes which are popular with women. *Greenshift* are a leaflet distribution agency which operates in the London area (they are listed in the Resource Directory at the back of this book).

Health centres were another good option, and this required a special letter to be written to the senior GP giving credentials (this is why it is not classed as 'free' - it costs time to do these letters and find out who to send them to, whereas putting a leaflet up on your local library notice board is something you can do en passant).

The cheapest sort of paid publicity is your own mailing list. If you don't have one, you can use someone else's, though it is always preferable to have your own. In this case, an excellent mailing list had already been compiled, and merely had to be updated asnd the press names checked. This particular list was well-targeted. Each batch of leaflets was sent with a polite note asking if the recipient would kindly display them (and quite a few other leafelts came swiftly back asking for the favour to be returned). Some of these duplicated those centres covered by the distribution service - and there's no harm in that. Others went to completely new venues.

By sheer co-incidence, one of the leaflets which came back was about a women's keep-fit week being held at four different centres in the area. All of these got added to the mailing list. Another last-minute addition was the local counselling network of 250. It only cost £10 to include the leaflet in the newsletter, and counsellors are good at mentioning colleagues' events to their clients, though they can't, of course, make them come. On this mailing lists were also all the local women's helplines, mainly for information, since women who ring such lines don't usually have the money to come to workshops. But the workers might.

PR (Public Relations) and Promotion

These are similar and different. Promotion includes giving free talks about your forthcoming workshop and rushing about exhibitions or fairs telling everyone you are doing it, and thrusting leaflets at them. Promotion also includes attendance at your chosen venue's open day, sending all your friends leaflets, and your family, and people you used to work with, and anyone else you can think of, as well as nonchalantly letting your existing clients see them. Note: if you are a psychotherapist, you need to discuss very carefully with your clients whether or not they want to come to your workshop, or tell their friends or partners about it. Clients have an image of you, and it can be quite disorienting to see you being someone different, and, indeed, giving your attention to so many other people. It is fine to send leaflets to former clients, the centre where you trained, your supervisor and your own therapist (if you have one) as well as to your professional association, insurance company, bank and anyone else who is interested in your career.

In this case, the free talk and the rushing about were done. The unusual extra was the press release (which comes under PR, though to doctors it means 'per rectum', so avoid the use of it at all costs.) The press release for this workshop was a bit of a scam, as to reiterate what was on the leaflet would not have been a press release at all. The idea was to think up an 'angle'. The end result was highly effective in 'PR' terms. One article to write, all the required listings, a mention in a care workers' weekly, and a local paper interview. Even if it wasn't published, the press release did its required job.

The press release was sent to women's editors (obviously), health editors, and listings editors of relevant newspapers, magazines and the local radio station. Two copies of the leaflet were included. One, unfolded, stapled to the back of the release. The other, folded as for display, tucked in the envelope. This was done because journalists either lose or throw away bits of paper which fall out of envelopes because they can't find the rest of the contents in the envelope; also because someone else in the office might pick it up, which in this case actually happened.

Results

Workshop participants per week
Week 1: 5 participants
Week 2: 10 participants
Week 3: 11participants*
Week 4: 10 participants
Week 5: 6 participants:
Week 7: 8 participants
Week 8: 8 participants
*would have been 14, but a storm and floods caused public transport chaos.

Moral 1: always get fees in advance.
Moral 2: plan well in advance
Moral 3: don't set fees too low

Comments: This was a good idea. A new and purposeful way of approaching a holistic workshop, with a specifically-targeted client group, a well-written and reasonably well-designed leaflet and an unusual colour, though there should have been 6,000 leaflets, instead of 3,000. Since the main point of the workshop, what made is unique, was the practical application of holistic techniques for *specific problems,* the fact that the problems weren't mentioned in the advertising meant that these told only half the story. This mistake was even more obvious from the fact that it was the leaflets which produced the clients, though the advertising did result in some enquiries. The publicity campaign was well thought out, though much of it was last-minute and more by luck and good instinct (plus experience) than careful planning.

The biggest mistake was allowing so little time for advance publicity, which led to buying more advertising space than was appropriate for this sort of workshop. It was a good example of a clear expression of the therapist's character, interests and typical way of working, though the little elements of cunning were not obvious in the leaflet and, therefore, hopefully not to the clients. The purpose for the therapist, to make money, clearly was unlikely to be fulfilled. More money would have been made by targetting a similar workshop to men and women rather than women only, and charging a higher fee, say £150 for the series (the cost of an expensive weekend workshop). If it had been possible to have twelve workshops this would have meant little additional publicity costs and therefore a bigger profit. To have achieved the initial target of 20 women, 10,000 leaflets, distributed to a geographically wider area, would have been necessary.

The real purpose was to create work for the therapist and to publicise herself at the new venue. In this way, the workshop series was highly successful, though the local newspaper article would have been a huge boost, had it appeared. The major things learnt were: fees had to be taken in advance and set at a higher rate. Planning, PR and promotion needed to be done earlier.

A word of encouragement... for people who feel complete failures.

Never mind if nothing works. Never mind if you've done all this and no-one ever comes. The universe has other plans for you. Life is full of surprises. People do not ignore all your publicity; they often sit on it, don't need you yet. A year or more later, they contact you and ask you to do something else. Do it. All publicity is good publicity. Things lead to other things. I have had this experience myself, countless times. Here is an example: I sent my cartoon book round to national newspapers for review and got nowhere. Several months later, a national daily health page editor rang and asked me if I could write a feature on co-dependence.

Many therapists who advertise in magazines say that they may get phone calls a year or more later. Those who advertise workshops or courses get asked for individual sessions. Osteopaths get asked to give talks. Environmental networks occasionally contact holistic practitioners for talks. Health clubs occasionally run workshops or staff training sessions.

Just as famous conductors *always* say they got their big break when an even more famous conductor had to cancel a concert because of illness, there are plenty of opportunities for practitioners to fill gaps. If, for instance, you are doing a workshop at one of the big festivals, check every morning if one of the other speakers has cancelled. As you probably earn half the receipts, it is worth the phone calls.

Once you are 'known', whether it is because you work in a Centre, or because you have distributed leaflets everywhere, or written an article for the local paper, or however you have promoted yourself, people begin to realise who you are. I have said this before, but it is really worth emphasising: it is not so much what you *do,* it is *who you are* that counts.

Final Words

If you are not doing what is right for you, it is a waste of you. This includes tackling your own marketing and publicity. This book will tell you everything you need to know, and even if you don't want to do it all yourself, the knowledge will also be useful for making sure the people who do your work for you, are doing it properly.

When you trained as a practitioner you probably did not realise the vast amount of work that is required to run a self-employed business. If you do not want to do the marketing and promotion then you could consider paying someone else to do it, if that's what you prefer. You may not even have to pay for it. You could set up a co-operative, for example, and share skills with others. There are things you do have to buy, such as printing and postage stamps. However if you know enough people you can offer reflexology in exchange for envelope stuffing, or for someone writing your leaflet, or hire a marketing guru to draw up a plan for you in exchange for a free place on your next 30 workshops. The only problem here is that what you produce will not be exactly 'you'. If this does not matter (e.g. you are only aiming for one-off clients) then it doesn't matter. However if you feel you matter then you will probably want to have a go yourself. The thing to remember is not to waste money. People's most common mistake, when they are unsure of themselves, is to overdo things. You don't need to buy a full page advertisement in a national newspaper for a workshop for 12 people in Cheam. Know your own abilities and know your own limits. If you want to learn more about any of the practical skills described in this book, there are affordable design and print courses at adult education centres. If you are on benefits, or a new business grant, you should be able to attend such courses very cheaply, sometimes even free. All the information you could possibly want is available. All you have to do is ask.

Remember that everything is connected, everything leads to something else, everything is a learning experience, everything you do is going to be valued by somebody. You are here on this planet because people need you. Good luck in finding your special place.

Resources

Mailing Lists

If you need to send your brochure/ leaflet to individuals or organisations in the holistic health/ New Age field, we have a range of mailing lists on offer. Our laser printed address labels are high quality at a very affordable price.

BCM Raft, London WC1N 3XX
(071) 733 7883 or fax (071) 978 9062
serving holistic business

Who are we?

Brainwave is a publisher and marketing specialist serving the Holistic health/New Age field. We serve publishers of books, audio and visual tapes, product suppliers and holistic health centres.

Trade Directory (USA)

Brainwave are agents for 'First Editions' a publishing company in the USA that produces a trade directory for the holistic health/New Age field. Our own trade directory is based on their excellent guide to the USA New Age marketplace. We have both volumes of this directory for sale.

Guidebooks

We publish two guidebooks aimed at the public who are interested in the holistic health/New Age field. This book *Holistic London*, now in it's third edition is packed with information on psychotherapy, alternative medicine and spiritual centres in the capital, as well as a list of resources including bookshops, products etc. It's an easy to use guidebook which has stood the test of time and is the only book of its kind for London. *The Whole Person Catalogue* is new and is destined to be the definitive nationwide guide to this growing field.

Co-operative Mailings

We mail out on a regular basis to individuals and businesses in the holistic health/ New Age field. If you wish to reach this specialist market we can include your brochure/leaflet in our mailings. This is a cost effective way to promote yourself. You simply supply the leaflets and we take care of the rest. We have regular mailouts to *retailers, centres, core advertisers and the general public.*

Marketing Packages

We supply marketing packages. Each package enables you to easily reach your chosen target group. It contains a set of labels and a description of each organisation on the label. Simply read the information we supply on an organisation, and if they are someone you wish to reach, then stick the appropriate label on to the envelope containing your book/product/press release/ brochure etc and post. Some packages we offer are *Reviewers Package, Press Release Package, Exhibitions Package, Core Advertisers Package, Publications Package,* and *Submissions Package.* The *Reviewers Package* is handy for publishers, audio and visual producers, and product suppliers who wish to promote their new book, product etc. The *Press Release Package* is useful for anyone wishes to mail off their press release, (we supply details of specialist and national press). The *Exhibitions Package* consists of details of holistic exhibitions so that you can plan ahead. The *Core Advertisers Package* consists of advertisers that advertise regularly in the MBS/New Age press; useful for those who wish to get advertising for their publication. The *Submissions Package* is for authors wishing to get their work published.

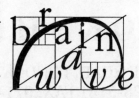